You GOT THIS!

TIPS FOR WOMEN WHO WANT TO ROCK AT REAL ESTATE INVESTING

Join the Women's Real Estate Network Community
www.facebook.com/wreninspires
www.instagram.com/wreninspires

Share your testimonials, comments, questions, breatkthroughs, successes and more.

Also receive your special bonuses for buying You Got This!
Go to www.WRENinspires.com/YouGotThis

You

GOT THIS!

TIPS FOR WOMEN WHO WANT TO ROCK AT REAL ESTATE INVESTING

by The Women's Real Estate Network
Publisher, Deborah Razo

Featuring
Jen Maldonado, Iris Veneracion, Kaaren Hall, Christina Suter,
Terri Garner and Alia Carter, Jennie Steed, Dawn Rickabaugh,
Maria Anderson and Kathryn Morea.

Dedication

I am truly thankful to all the people over the years who helped me make the decision to become a real estate investor and then backed it up by educating, supporting and basically keeping me going. Without them I might never have known how great life can be!

To my family and friends, thank you for your prayers and supporting me during the darkest days and for telling me that I had the power to change my life and that I could be whatever I wanted to be. Without you all I don't know where I would be. I love you.

And thank you to all the women who come out to our meetings and events. This wouldn't be possible without you!

To Jessica, Matthew and Rick, thank you for giving me the courage to be whatever I wanted to be. You are my greatest strength and love.

Acknowledgments

To Sandra Rea our managing editor for your hours making this book happen. And to Karla Olivares for your contributions as a project manager for keeping us on track with such grace. To Dori, for making this happen so quickly!

And of course to all the women that contributed to this book. You are amazing and I'm so happy to be able to share your experiences with others out there. Thank you for your continued encouragement and support.

WREN
WOMEN'S REAL ESTATE NETWORK
www.WRENinspires.com

Table of Contents

Introduction

If you are reading these words, you're probably a woman who is either actively involved in real estate investing or you have been wondering how to participate in some way. You are eager to learn new things and you're really interested in how you can earn passive income through real estate investments.

You may have heard of a few strategies, like wholesaling or flipping, but you want to learn more. You crave the education. You want to learn from other women who have been where you are right now.

Maybe your understanding of real estate is deeper because you are a more seasoned investor, and you're wondering what it would be like to own a multifamily property, a whole apartment building or perhaps a piece of commercial real estate.

If that describes you, whether you're a newbie or well-seasoned as an investor, you are reading the right book. I put it together for you, to support you in your journey as a real estate entrepreneur and investor. If that's you, you're going to love reading this book and learning from the variety of female investors we interviewed!

What gives me the credentials to write this book?

Fair question! To begin with I have been investing in real estate for several years and have stood exactly where you are right now. As time marched on, I gained new skills, starting with one deal and working my way up to bigger and bigger deals. Today I am a real estate developer, educator and coach. Plus, I founded WREN, the Women's Real Estate Network!

My name is Deborah Razo and I welcome you to read the stories that I've collected in the pages of this book. These are stories of other women's journeys in the real estate investing world. Just like WREN, this is a collective where you will find inspiration, motivation and guidance into various strategies and all the wonderful things you can accomplish through investing in real estate! By the time you've finished reading all the stories you will see that there are so many ways to earn a living in real estate that it could make your head spin. I've come to know these contributors well because they have been women to have inspired, advised and effected my real estate journey.

If you aren't familiar with WREN I won't hold it against you. We have a simple objective. To create a community where women in real estate can come together, share their experiences, excel as investors and empower each other. We have worked hard to create a safe space where all women involved in real estate investing, as well as those who are just now beginning their journey, can openly and fearlessly share their experiences, resources and tools to help one another grow both personally and professionally. Plus, we get to have a whole lot of FUN doing it!

How did WREN come to be?

While my story is the first in this book, I can summarize WREN's beginnings here.

WREN sprang from my imagination after I had been in real estate for a while and attending real estate investing education and networking events. Just like you, I was looking for presenters at the front of the room with whom I could identify. The interesting thing is that I hadn't seen a lot of women at the front of the room! Sure, I had received a lot of great real estate education, but mostly from men in the industry. While they had great information to share I found that I couldn't truly identify with them. Truth is that they likely couldn't identify with the women in the room either.

For example, did these men have an internal alarm that went off every day at 3pm because they'd been programmed over the years to wonder if their children were getting picked up on time from school? Did they ever experience feelings of guilt or anxiety for working when they felt they should be home with their children PLUS feelings of guilt or anxiety when they were with their kids thinking they should be working? That's pretty much a woman thing.

I know this to be true because I am a woman and I've experienced those thoughts. So have a lot of women I've spoken with about it. I remember sitting in the audience at real estate investing events, wondering what was going on in a man's head as I watched him speak at the front of the room and try to sell expensive courses at the back of the room.

More and more I found myself craving a different educational and networking experience.

WREN was born!

In an effort to find "my peeps," my group of real estate investors and interested others, I first reached out to women in my community. Why not get a bunch of Los Angeles Women real estate investors together for a Sunday brunch, right?

So I invited women who work full-time as real estate investors. Many RSVP'd and we were off to the races! The first meeting of WREN would soon be under way.

Since we were a small group of female entrepreneurs, we weren't going to have your typical, boring business meetup. Not by a long shot. First, we met on a Sunday afternoon. That was different. Second, we drank champagne and we talked about life, real estate, and all that we enjoyed in our personal and professional lives. In other words, it wasn't just a meeting of likeminded individuals; it was a way to get to really get to know each other.

This first WREN meeting happened in downtown Los Angeles. There are now five chapters spread across a couple of states, and we're getting ready to expand into more! You can read about that in my chapter of this book.

From that first meeting to what WREN continues to become is an ever-growing network of women who join for the purpose of helping each other solve problems. We share resources with each other all the time and generally empower each other inside and outside our meetings and events.

At the end of that first brunch I asked for the attendees' input about my ideas about WREN and what I intended. Their response was overwhelming and to this day I can remember the warmth I felt in that room! When I told them I wanted to have a meetup every quarter, their response was more than a collective YES. They wanted me to host more meetings.

Wow. Now that's what I call validation! That's how the Women's Real Estate Network began. The rest is history... which is something we're still making. We met every other month for awhile and, yes, there was usually wine involved. Moreover, we continued to network with each other, share resources and our experiences in real estate investing, and we also shared a whole lot of laughter.

What began as a casual Sunday afternoon brunch has turned into a community of female entrepreneurs in real estate who enjoy the friendship, advice and comradery that comes with being part of something bigger than ourselves. Once I realized there were a great number of women in the country that could benefit from this network, WREN became an official brand. With the help of my friend and colleague Jen Maldonado, I started the official Los Angeles WREN Meetup.

Next thing you know, we were asking seasoned female rock stars in real estate to speak at our meetings, because the women in the audience were sure to benefit from their knowledge and experiences. Many of the members were already investors who wanted to up their game. An equal number were new to real estate investing altogether and they attended our meetings to learn new things and choose a path. Either way, they would benefit from our presenters!

Women started to show up to the meetings in greater and greater numbers. Some drove quite a distance to get to the meetings and for a variety of different reasons. From stay-at-home moms looking for a way to afford a private school for their children or family vacations to single moms looking to learn how to turn real estate investing into a way to create or replace their full-time income to women who had been doing deals in real estate for years, WREN's membership is incredibly diverse.

Why don't you join us next time?

If you've been looking for a place to network and grow, and if you are willing to ask for help from those doing what you want to do in real estate investing, WREN is a safe place where you can do all of that and more.

It is my dream that women understand the value of having a space where they can come together to collaborate, where they don't have to feel alone in any difficult deals or situations in real estate, and where they don't have to feel intimidated to ask for help, get resources, gain knowledge and maybe even have a lot fun along the way.

Today, joining WREN is easier than ever before. Like I mentioned earlier, we now have five chapters with monthly meetings in Los Angeles, Seattle, Orange County, Phoenix and San Diego. We are also expanding into more cities and states. So why not join us?

You will leave our events energized and ready to take on the next big deal! We want you to thrive in real estate investing, which means you'll have to change your mindset and let new ideas percolate. Let WREN help motivate you to achieve greater personal and business success than you dared dream possible.

Learn more. Visit www.WRENinspires.com!

But first, read this book.

In its pages you will meet real rock stars in the women's real estate investing space. I'm sure you'll connect with their stories. After all, these are real people who've gone through the paces in real estate investing. They've gained, lost and built up again.

Why?

- They are resilient.

- They are intelligent.

- They are sensitive.

- They ask a lot of questions.

- They move forward boldly, putting their fears aside.

- They are female entrepreneurs!

Now let's turn to the next page both here and in life?

I invite you to get to know these wonderful women of WREN!

Enjoy,
Deborah Razo

"I met a real estate investor who was in her 80s who knew everything going on with her properties. I want to be that woman when I'm in my 80s, still involved in real estate investing, still working the deals!"

~Deborah Razo, WREN Founder, Real Estate Developer

Deborah Razo, Founder, Women's Real Estate Network (WREN)

All heart and a lot of hard work

As the founder of the Women's Real Estate Network (WREN), Deborah Razo says she continues to put her heart into expanding her organization nationwide.

"WREN is a heart thing for me," she says. "And it's been a pretty exciting adventure, too. What's really exciting is that now I get to work with some amazing rock stars in real estate investing. You'll get to hear their stories. When you're done, you'll see what I mean about these women. But first, I hope you take a few minutes to read my story."

***

I've been an entrepreneur for 20+ years. Entrepreneurship is not for the faint of heart. It requires taking calculated risks, learning to live with uncertainty and putting in a lot of hard work, just to mention a few things. Ten years ago I got an "opportunity to start over." Anyone ever have one of those? Mine was in the form of a severe car accident that literally changed my life. You hear that phrase in your life, but it doesn't mean much until something happens to you. In this accident a tire blew and my girlfriend lost control of the car. In a matter of seconds the car flipped. I was on the passenger side and received the brunt of the collision.

I was rushed to the hospital with a head wound that needed immediate attention and within 24 hours was told I had a broken neck! You might think that would be the end of my take, but as it happens, this was actually an opportunity to start over in my life. After all, I had a year to recover and a whole lot of time to think about what I really wanted out of my life.

Was I living the life that I even wanted? How could I change the parts I didn't like? Over time I came to realize that I was spending more time with my computer than I was with other human beings and the people that meant a lot to me in my life. This time tested my faith and I knew that something had to change.

It was shocking to realize that my primary relationship was with my computer! What I really wanted was more time with my family, time to travel and just time to enjoy my life. That was the turning point. I knew I'd have to get busy changing my life and my story.

The problem was that I didn't know how to change.

While I started and ran my own business, in reality I was really just self-employed, trading my time for money. Wow! That was an eye-opener.

During my recovery, my brother came to take care of me. I'm grateful to him, because he helped me discover what this major life event really meant to me. It was a journey of faith in God, accepting help and support from others and realizing I had the power to change my life. My brother supported that if I wanted to change my life I had the power to do it. Boy, was he ever right! So I started studying different ways to earn a living.

When I could walk again, I attended life-changing events. For example, I enjoyed attending Tony Robbins' events where I could learn how to change my mindset. That was great, but I didn't stop there. Suffice it to say that I became a master Google researcher. I had many questions; Google had answers!

More than anything, I wanted to know how to earn passive income. That's something I had heard a lot about and, during searches online, I kept landing on real estate investing as an answer. In the end, I did more searching online and in the real world, this time to find a mentor and educator who told me that I need to develop an investment philosophy and then draw up a plan. So that's what I did. For a long time I flipped for capital and I would reinvest the capital into longer-term cashflowing properties to create wealth.

I loved the life I was creating!

I can't tell you how much time I've spent looking at Redfin, Zillow and all those other places that had great properties for the taking. It was clear that I wanted to be involved in real estate investing.

I realized if you want to be successful in real estate investing – or really anything at all – you have to be genuinely interested in what you're investing in. There it was... I was off and running. I would earn income through investing in real estate.

My first investment was with a partner who taught me what I needed to know about flipping successfully, including how to putting hard money in place and how to handle construction of a flip. That partner was an amazing teacher and mentor.

If there were one thing I could tell somebody just starting out in real estate investing today, it would be to work with someone who has been doing what you want to do for at least a couple of years. Learn from that person. Then you can go off and try it on your own. That's what I did and it worked pretty well!

When I was well-versed in flipping, I bought my first turnkey buy-and-hold property, which I rented out to tenants. This was in Memphis. Once I became experienced in real estate, I realized I could buy properties in Memphis, fix them up and then flip them or keep them, and put tenants in place. I learned that I would need to put a team together to help, so that's what I did. I didn't think about it too much; in fact, I moved quickly. No analysis paralysis here!

Had I stopped to ponder and think, think, think about it I may not have pulled the trigger. I had put more thought into the end result. I wanted more rental properties, so I would invest in a fixer, flip it and then use the profits to buy a new rental properties. That became my system.

Fast forward to today and you'll find that I am a developer. Crazy, huh? While I never set out to be one, it's my latest adventure. And it's pretty exciting. I've tried other strategies yet always return to flipping, which if you think about it has a lot of similarities to what it takes to develop properties. I just love the whole experience of taking something ugly, using my skills to make it pretty and then making everyone money in the process.

For me, flipping (and developing) fit my personality and goals. I figured I would stay with flipping forever, but one day I met a really cool female developer, a real standout named Beth Clifford. Later I met another woman developer named Linday Wishard at a Seattle WREN Chapter event. She simplified things for me, telling me, "When flipping you are taking on unseen problems. With developing you're not. Developing requires upfront paperwork, but when you get the go-ahead from all the entities involved, like the city you build it up and it's great."

Hey, she was absolutely right! Developing takes a lot longer than flipping a property, but in the end the rewards are greater.

I opened myself to learning more. Over time, I met my partner, a person who really knows the ropes when it comes to developing properties. I employed the same process of learning how to become a developer that I used when entering the market as a flipper. By that I mean taking a partner from whom I could learn because that person had been developing properties a long time.

Partnerships can be a great way to learn a lot quickly. So that's what I did, and I'm really happy about my choice. My partner's name is Marietta Andersen (check out her chapter in the book) out of Los Angeles. Her company name is the Ando Group in case you want to Google her!

I have learned a lot from Maria (that's how we endearingly call her), like how everything costs more than projected, that you have to get into the details and jump through a lot of hoops when you're working with the city, and that developing properties is definitely a team sport. There's just no way you can be a lone wolf in this area of investing.

At the time of this writing, I'm at the demolition phase in a property we are developing. By the time you read this I will be well into the project. As a developer I've learned that you are the quarterback of the team, keeping the project and the team on track.

When I first got into real estate investing I heard things that could have scared me away. Some were true and some were not. For example, I heard that you just can't do it alone. I agree. You can't! At least not if you want to build your property portfolio, and especially if you want to build it quickly.

A team may not be what you're thinking. For instance, I need a property manager to run my rental properties. Whether it's a person or a whole property management company, that person or company is essential in running my properties. There's a lot to that job, and there's no way I could do all of it on my lonesome

You're always going to have to network. You will never stop growing that network. That way you'll find the right people to work with in different deals. In different properties. In different strategies.

Team-building isn't the only thing I learned we need as investors. When I first got into real estate investing I didn't think I'd need communication skills. Boy, was I wrong! Real estate investing requires good communication skills.

Before I was a real estate investor I was fairly isolated in my work, and I made decisions on my own. I didn't work with teams of people like I do today. There's a quote I like a lot: "Real estate is simple but not easy." That couldn't be truer. That's why you need people (a.k.a., a team) and good communication skills.

Take WREN, for example. That was a result of a few months of banging my head against a wall trying to get my next deal. I wanted to know how others were doing it and wondered where are all women were. I found them! And what an inspiration. Learning about what the women who were in the industry were doing, how they find properties and how they run their businesses.

Men and women do operate differently. That's part of the reason I'm writing this book.

I find it intriguing how women tend to work from a place of passion and with a lot of heart.

Looking back at our first WREN meeting I have to smile. It was just a simple brunch where a few women got together to discuss challenges they were experiencing in their deals and properties. We helped each other and it felt great. We shared resources. Then we decided that we should do this thing every month. That way we wouldn't feel so alone. We were able to come together and share advice, give each other support, and just encourage each other to do what was necessary to reach our goals. I realized during those early meetings that there were other women who wanted to learn more about investing. They didn't know amazing rock star real estate investors who are also women who were doing what they wanted to do. It was clear that I needed to get the introductions going.

WREN was born from a simple meetup in Los Angeles and now we have five chapters! I'm happy to say that we have L.A., Seattle, Orange County, Phoenix, and San Diego. We are expanding and absolutely exploding onto the scene! At the time of this writing we're looking at three more cities and the U.S. where we will add chapters. I can't wait to let you know where the next chapters will be.

As our network grows I can call members in other markets who will share their resources with me. That was just a vision just a few short years ago and now it is reality. As a woman-only organization, we cater to the novice and the seasoned investor alike who need questions answered and want to share their experiences in real estate investing. As women, we all love to share our knowledge; newbies love the experience of being surrounded by so many women who are out there doing deals and making things happen.

If you are reading this and you have not yet started doing deals or maybe you haven't yet dipped your toe into much education on the various strategies you can use to create wealth through real estate investing, the first thing you need to do is sit with yourself. Figure out what you want to do in real estate. Then you need to find a partner who is seasoned in that area of investing. If you have to give away more of the profit in your first couple of deals that's just fine. This will allow you to move ahead with other deals and by then you'll know what you're doing. Think of it in terms of your getting paid to learn!

To the woman looking to up their game, someone who is a bit seasoned and already investing who may be looking at different strategies, it is best to surround yourself with stronger peers in different areas of investing. You want to surround yourself with people who are really taking it to the next level in real estate investing! If you surround yourself with peers who are above your level of understanding that's great. All the better! There's true value in this approach; it sure makes me push myself. Surround yourself with those individuals you want to emulate. (Not just women either.)

I like working with women in real estate investing because I've noticed that they tend to give back more. Not just to their communities, but to each other at networking events. They want to share their knowledge. They like helping other women get further ahead. I should know; I am one!

Women don't really look at real estate investing and finance the same way as men. In my opinion, the language of business was created by men. Can we speak that language? Sure. But why do we need to? Our language as women is more collaborative and intuitive, plus we make decisions differently. We tend to take more time making our decisions. Another difference between men and women is that we are not afraid to ask for help or guidance. It's like stopping to ask for directions when you're lost in the car. Women will do it, but men typically won't.

Like everyone in real estate, I've encountered plenty of challenges. Shoot, I have them all the time. As an entrepreneur I've found that if my phone isn't ringing things are going pretty well. Of course, it's okay if the phone does ring. Problems are there to be handled.

As an investor you will learn to handle problems. You might even get to where you enjoy being a problem solver. I find joy in it; when someone calls me with a problem and I can give them a new perspective it makes my day. That happens all the time. I try not to get off the phone until we have come up with three options or three solutions. If I were to just give one option or one solution that's not enough!

I jokingly say that my phone only rings if there is a problem. When everything is running smoothly I don't hear from people. That's where having a good network built of strong relationships can be part of the solution.

Everything in real estate is about relationships, especially when it comes to investing. Let's say you own properties far from where you live and work. This long-distance investing will require you to develop very strong relationships with your team that is helping you manage the prop- erties. That's going to require a whole lot of phone calls. It's been said that I give a really good phone! But talking on the phone didn't come naturally to me; it was something I had to learn.

I'm always learning. I'm guessing I won't ever stop. There will be a lot of turns and stops along my journey! The path that led me to where I am today was not exactly a straight line, but then it never really is, is it? If you speak to any seasoned investor you'll see that this is very true. And they will all tell you to become a creative problem-solver.

For example, one of my flip properties was tented for termites. Just when I thought things were going well we found that there was a beehive in one of the walls. When we opened that wall we found a 3.5-foot bee hive, the bees had died in the tenting and the smell was horrible. Rotted honey! After putting on my problem-solver cap, I had a beekeeper come out to remove the hive right way. You may wonder how the bees got in there. We learned they came in through a venting system from the outside and had been building their hive for several years. I never saw the hive neither did my inspectors. It just happened.

In another situation I had a problem getting through inspections on a property. We didn't do things in the right order. But I didn't know any different. Call it another learning opportunity.

My partner and I were rehabbing a three-bedroom, one-bath property, turning it into a four-bedroom, two-bath property. In that project we did a little work before the inspector came out. Because we didn't do things in the right order he made is take down everything we'd done, which slowed the process immensely. In flipping, time equals money. We lost weeks in that project. But we worked through the issues. That wasn't really all that long ago, and at the time of this writing we are clipping along again. All I can say is that I learned something very important and that's to call the inspector before you start any work and see what he needs first before you take another step. That can save you a whole lot of time, effort and money.

I wasn't always able to solve problems as well as I do today. Sure, I've been the decision-maker in my work, but as I mentioned earlier I didn't have to look to other people to help me figure out how to get beyond challenges. Sometimes I made great decisions; sometimes I didn't.

I've had a long and varied background in different industries. And I have gone through some adversities in my life. Remember the car wreck that started my story? Heck, we have all been through hard times, right? What I've learned over the years is that getting through adversities is just a matter of perspective.

Take a page from my book. When I am frustrated, scared, worried and wake up at 4:00 AM torturing myself with all that could be's and what if's, I play game. I call it the "Equal Time Game"! Here's how it works...

If I spend time focusing on how things can go wrong, I have to give equal time to what can go right. The reason I came up with this strategy, which I hope helps you too, is because I couldn't stop overthinking bad possible outcomes for my projects, even when they were going well. I had to do something. Because I couldn't stop that nonsense in my head, I thought maybe I could mitigate it.

When I first started this game it was really hard. Try it sometime!

For example, when I told myself that I had to think of all that good stuff that was going on in a project or in my life, it was like crickets up there in my head. Over time I got better at thinking of the positives and became a better problem-solver as a result. Now I work that into my coaching sessions. This method is very helpful to my clients, and maybe it will help you, too.

Being involved in real estate investing is a point of joy in my life. Starting WREN is another.

WREN has brought me the most joy ever! It became a really cool opportunity for opening women's eyes to all the possibilities waiting for them in real estate investing. Running WREN can be very challenging some days, and I never saw myself as a front-of-the-room type of person, but here I am. (Truth be told, I was more of a back-of-the-WREN heckler.)

Today, when I hear of the successes that members are having that's a real win for me personally. One woman in particular comes to mind. Karen, a woman who owns a salon had been investing in rental property with her husband. Truth is that her husband was primarily managing the properties while she ran the salon. Sadly her husband suddenly died and she found support and guidance in WREN to keep going. The end result was she succeeded in her projects and found a group of networking resources.

That's what WREN is all about. It brings us as women together so that we can give back and share and just help each other. We all need support and as women we are able to do that for each other. In that way, you will reach your financial goals through investing.

If you're looking for financial successes in all of your deals that's a really great. I love it. But that's not going to happen overnight. It is a journey. Getting there is definitely a team sport. Enjoy the journey.

As I look down the road, maybe 20 years from now I'm sure I'll still be involved in real estate and WREN.

Recently, I spoke to an 80-something-year-old woman who was selling her multifamily building. She was incredible! I really like this woman, because she knew everything about her building. The woman knew all the details about running this building. She was liquidating her portfolio due to her husband's illness. She was at a stressful point in her life and needed to cash out some of her properties. In the end we both got what we wanted, which is exactly what you do in real estate investing.

I got off that phone call and thought... That will be me when I'm in my eighties! I'll keep working because it makes me happy.

I think of real estate investing kind of like surfing. I don't surf, but when things get bigger in my mind than I think I can handle, I imagine if I were a surfer and just ride the wave.

I may not know how I'm getting to shore, but the ride is pretty cool. I just think let's see where this thing... this project... lands!

That way when I get freaked out, like when things go wrong in a deal, I can turn my thinking around. I get excited about the outcome. Remember the game I mentioned earlier? The "Equal Time Game"? That's what you have to do and surf that wave to shore.

As a result of my involvement in real estate investing my personal life has improved dramatically. I have more flexibility now I've ever had before. Building wealth is a goal and it is a process, but investing in properties will get you there. I may not be completely out of the rat race yet, but now I have a lot more time to get there. Every morning when I wake up it's a new day and there will be new opportunities. Every month I'm looking at different properties and I'm running different projects, but it's not just to build my wealth; it is also to build a legacy.

What I'm doing now is more than just real estate investing. I'm working to improve communication and all my relationships, which includes my relationship with my fiancé and my two children. I'm working on building better and stronger relationships with my friends, too. The way I see it, being involved in real estate investing is a lifelong endeavor. We should never stop working on building the best relationships!

THREE TIPS:

[1] **Network!** Find out what others are doing, how they are operating, how they are finding deals and everything else you can think of. See how you can help other people get to their goals, which helps you get to yours. Networking is all about support and sharing experiences. Without networking your ship can sink pretty quickly.

[2] **Learn how to run numbers.** Early on I would get emotional about investments. But you can't do that. Stick to the numbers. Look at the profitability of your projects. This is not the house that you're going to move into and live in. It's not a building that you're going to live in either. These properties that you are buying are investments. Treat them as such. Remove the emotionality from your deals.

[3] **Come up with multiple exit strategies, even if your project is a flip.** This is something I understand well. Let's say I'm doing a flip and we run into problems. Maybe it can't be flipped for a good profit. You need to come up with a different strategy for the property. For example, could it be a rental? Could it be an independent living home for elders who can still take care of themselves to a certain degree? Could it be an assisted living home? Could it be a sober living home? What could that be? How can you change the use of that property to make good cashflow until such time that you can sell it? It could be that if you develop a business inside of that property that you can also sell at exit for more money because the buyer will want to take you up on that opportunity. Think about it!

You GOT THIS!

"I praise women I've met along the way who've influenced me to be an influencer myself and a leader that can impact other women's lives."

~ Jennifer Maldonado, REI Influencer

Jennifer Maldonado, Real Estate Entrepreneur

Always engineer the best deals

When Jennifer Maldonado was a young girl, her mother asked her what she wanted to be when she grew up. You might think she'd say a veterinarian, a teacher or any number of jobs a lot of girls think about, but instead she said she wanted to have the best job ever. Jennifer answered, "I want to work in a chocolate factory and at a baby lotion factory!"

Jennifer, connected the dots later in life and discovered that her dreams became true. She worked at Johnson & Johnson and then for Nestle, so she got pretty close. However, after working a number of years in her jobs earning a great income she noticed that the long hours and stress played havoc with her personal life. Something had to change, so she struck out to find a new path. This is Jennifer's story...

***

What I did in my professional life seemed to always take center stage. It wasn't just that the hours were long, but rather I didn't take much time for a personal life. I put my career and professional aspiration first getting in the way of relationships. Even so, I thought I had met a man who understood me and who was a real partner who would really support my endeavors and my work ethics. He promised me Heaven and filled me with great hopes. He had other plans. Later I would realize he was more focused on my earnings and what he could get from our relationship for his personal advancement and bragging rights than on a future together. After all, I had earned a six-figure income by the age of 25 with no debt, a simple life and not much needed to feel fulfilled and certain about success. I had worked hard for that money and become a person of value while he was hanging out with his friends until sunrise. In the end his intentions and desire to get everything in his favor was also the end of us as a couple. My mother warned me to be careful. She didn't approve and neither did my real friends. I lost myself in the journey of this

You GOT THIS!

relationship. That was about the time I decided my life had to change and that I needed more freedom.

As a result of my broken heart, I isolated myself and fell into a long depression period, lost contact with my friends and family, and I lost passion for a lot of things in life that until then I had truly loved. My confidence, faith and courage that drive me for many years, suddenly were just a hidden treasure.

It took me three years to get him out of my life and even my relationship ended up in a court battle. Talk about dark moments. I'm sharing this with you because I want you to know that no matter how bleak things look at times, as long as we keep breathing there is always a solution. We just don't know it yet. And sometimes the "bad" things we go through are getting us ready for the brightest future we are destined to create. For example, the relationship issues I went through. I had to go through that messy journey to get to where I am today, because it is during the dark times... the dark moments... in our lives when we ask ourselves what we really want and who we want to become. For me that was a time of awakening and enlightenment.

After putting thought and heart into my next steps, I decided what I wanted to do. For me, it was important to be back on top, but now I wanted to do it my way and not just be a high-paid cog in a corporate wheel earning money for the company. That was a pivotal decision, especially when you think about when I made it. The year was 2013 and I was at the top of my career. Plus, I had just received my biggest promotion to date. It was also the time I put in my notice. Something in me said it was time. While I was very excited about my unsure future, I have to admit that I was scared to death.

That was several years ago and I've learned a lot of new skills. Today I raise capital for multiple equity projects. This was within my plan for my new life; I would just have to figure out how I was going to get there! At that time I didn't know much about raising capital or about real estate investing. That meant I had a lot of intensive classes ahead of me. I found a mentor with whom I could learn things about investing in multifamily properties and other strategies. Plus I took three months of coaching.

I'll have to thank my brother for suggesting that I take classes. He said that I can do anything. My mom and dad opposed completely to me adventuring into an entrepreneurship journey until today. That's why I didn't tell them that I quit my job until three months later. Looking back, I guess my brother was right! I am grateful for my two older brothers and all the encouragement that they gave me.

Classes and mentoring weren't all it took. I also became an avid reader of all things related to real estate investing. Like most other real estate investors and entrepreneurs, I read the purple book by Robert Kiyosaki. That book opened my eyes to a new way of earning a living outside the corporate world.

I took classes prior to handing in my resignation. Six months earlier, in fact. Most of these classes were taught by women. Because the classes were expensive, and I didn't have enough to cover them all, I asked to borrow money from my mom, even she didn't know which classes I was taking, I knew I had to pay for them. In essence, I was raising private capital for my education! In the end, I raised enough to cover two good classes. The interesting part is that I raised the money needed in 24 hours! If I hadn't I wouldn't have gotten in. When I did I couldn't believe it! It was thrilling to know I was on a new path. I did not know how it would all play out, but I'm real glad I took those classes.

A year later, my life would take another surprising turn. My mother was diagnosed with breast cancer in December of 2013. Not even a month after I had left my job, which meant I could spend time with my mother. In the end, she survived, but it made me realize just how fragile life is and how we all need to lead our life the way we want. For me, it meant throwing off the confines of the corporate entity that was running and possibly ruining my life.

At the time, however, I didn't really have a solid plan. I wasn't sure where I should keep my focus on real estate, so I started acquiring residential multi-family properties and non-performing notes, and learned how to raise capital. The cool thing is that the notes turned 20% profits in the first few months. Maybe I did so well because I worked with a partner who was teaching me these new skills.

That was a great lesson for me, so I began partnering with other people. I attended lots of networking events, too. At one event I met a creative real estate developer. I didn't really understand what that was at the time but it sounded like it was something I could work and learn. During those days I was struggling financially, but I didn't let that fact stop me from working with this man and we raised $700,000 for his project. That put me on a good path. In another 1.5 years I raised more than $1M for different deals. I have now raised enough money for other people to create portfolios with a total worth of $50,000,000! Now I'm ready to go the next level. My next phase will be to buy multifamily properties, using a value-add strategy to bump up cashflow and make them more profitable. It is important to me that these properties also benefit the neighborhoods where they are located. For example, I want to help veterans, seniors and disabled children.

The way I see it, we all have disabilities of one kind or another. But the kids I want to help are those with physical disabilities. This goes back to my days in college when I worked with the local 4H Club with friends. I was asked to be the leader of a summer camp for disabled children. What a learning experience this turned out to be! When I first got to the camp I had my own plans to do all sorts of things. Boy, I was going to teach these kids. What happened was quite the reverse. They taught me so much about life that I couldn't believe it. These kids were joyful no matter what their situation.

One child in my group was always talking to the other kids. I would watch him as he talked to his peers. They were listening and I felt humbled. This boy taught other kids how to overcome challenges they were facing in their lives. This was possibly the most impactful time of my life.

Today when I work with other people I think back to that time. I know how to help them. It comes from listening and sharing openly. I want to be the type a leader that disabled boy was, and I want to help other people who are just like him.

At the time of this writing I am in chats with community leaders in southern California's Inland Empire who have an organization that helps veterans and the disabled that need housing. I'm learning how to create specific housing for that target population. I get to work with the government, which is pretty exciting, and we are also looking at creating larger centers for the veterans and the disabled. In fact we're looking at 4-and 5-plexes, as well as hotels that we can convert.

Looking back, I could not have foreseen all that I'm involved with as a result of my decision to become a real estate investor. The reason I'm here is because I know my WHY.

When working with new investors I always ask them what their "why" is. What is it they are passionate about? Then I can help them figure out their strategy and they can focus on their short- and long-term goals.

Real estate investing has hundreds of possibilities. When I started out, I didn't even know what escrow was; the only thing I knew about it came from playing Monopoly as a child. I knew I'd have to network with those who know more than me. To optimize your success, you need to focus on a strategy that is in alignment with your goals. Knowing your "why" and surrounding yourself with people who know more than you do is the starting point.

It may take a while to figure things out. For example, I didn't know everything I know today about real estate investing, strategies, the different types of properties or even exit strategies when I first got into real estate. While I learned a lot from taking courses I learned more from people with whom I networked.

You'll find that not every strategy will work for you. In the beginning, I thought maybe flipping properties would be sexy so I learned all I could about it. After that I realized it wasn't for me. I didn't feel it was in alignment with who I am or with my goals.

If you've been into real estate for a little while and you're more of a seasoned investor you need to keep adding to your toolbox of skills. Keep getting educated. Don't think you can get to success on your own. Get help from others, keep networking and find mentors who know more than you do.

Maybe that's why so many people want to invest in the properties I'm involved in. My education and focus is apparent, which is a good thing. Like me, you'll learn as you grow and do more deals. But if you know someone who does something you're wanting to do in real estate, why not learn from them? Take notes. Lots of notes. I keep a journal of information and collect stories from people I meet. Then I can refer back to them when I need the information. It helps me to be prepared for different projects and strategies.

Whether you are new to real estate investing or you've been at it for a while, be smart with your time. Understand how to better assess where you are financially. That's one thing I really wish I had known in the beginning. That's why I created a free course for people who want to be involved in real estate investing. Here's a link to sign up for that free course: http://jenmaldonado.thinkific.com/

Another thing that every real estate investor or anybody interested in participating in any kind of deals should do is to play the Cashflow 101 board game. Created by Robert Kiyosaki, the game teaches you that what can be done on the board can be done in real life. This is not Monopoly. It isn't about ruling the board. Real estate investing takes a team effort. This game teaches you how to work with other people to get deals done, and then even bigger and bigger deals. I've used this game to teach others about what I do and what they can achieve through real estate investing. I can't recommend it highly enough! If you want to play, you can find lots of games in your area; just check online at Meetup.com and you'll see what I mean.

One last thing I'd say to anybody just getting into real estate investing and learning all the different strategies is to stay away from the syndrome of jumping into all the new shiny objects that you will come in contact with. It's easy to get sucked into every different strategy and not implement any. I choose to learn one strategy, implement it and, if I like it, just keep doing it. Right now, I choose a combination of earning big fat checks as private lender and developer, and also the deals that bring cashflow over the long-term like multi-family properties.

For the more seasoned investor I'd say you need to focus on creating a different mindset that will take you to the next level. You must network with other investors. That is not an option. These investors need to be at higher levels than you are so you can learn more than you know now. In this way you can also discover new opportunities. Plus you get to learn about different markets.

You must have clarity. That means you have to know your focus. You have to make a plan and stick to it. It is okay if you have to adjust along the way. For example, in my business sometimes we write a business plan. Writing things down is the first step. Writing your intentions down and writing your plan out on paper as specifically as you can is critical to your success.

Let's say you want a rehab 20 or 100 properties a month. Well, that means you need to have a plan that involves not just the projects but also the people, money and other resources you will need to get these projects done. If you want to grow, you'll have to prepare yourself for that growth. You'll have to leave your fears behind. Leave your experiences at the door until they are required. Get your creativity and imagination going to open yourself to new ways of thinking. In fact, you should think like a child, which means you're thinking about everything like its brand new, something you don't know. What's that old saying? You can't fill a cup that's already full. Be an empty cup.

Your plan needs to include how many properties you want to buy, but that's the easy part. You'll need to develop new habits and new practices to achieve the success you want. Collaborate with other women (and men) in real estate.

As women we tend to share openly so collaboration is easy, and we need to collaborate with other people a lot. That collaboration is key to our success. While we can certainly learn from men, we tend to learn better from other women. It's just how our brains work. We need to tap into our feminine energy.

I remember talking to a woman I met at a WREN event in Seattle. She was doing a lot of different projects and I was able to help her raise capital for her deals. Had I not been open to that opportunity, and had I not tapped into my feminine energy, I would not have been able to help her.

It's a good idea to put due dates on your plan so it gives the plan real life. This actually gives you more opportunities of contributing to the world. As a woman this is very important me to contribute to the world. Many women I've spoken with feel the same.

There's one thing I know for sure. Limits are imaginary. We can grow as big as we want and reach every goal we desire. We can help others grow, too, by networking and sharing openly with each other. I am living proof.

Maybe that's because I didn't listen to myths about investing. For example, I thought that you need a lot of money to operate in real estate investing successfully. You don't. You can use other people's money just as well as you can use your own. It's about learning how to get access to capital!

When I played Monopoly as a child with my father I told him I wanted to buy a lot of properties like the hotels on the board. What I didn't know to say is that I wanted to buy multifamily properties! He laughed and said

I would need a lot of money if I wanted to do that. He didn't know what he didn't know, and I had to learn this idea wasn't correct.

Later when I bought a duplex, I was still operating on that old ideal, so I tapped into my own 401K savings, living in one side while renting the other. When I learned how to raise private capital it really opened doors for me and I found quickly that I could do way bigger projects. That was exciting.

Another myth I heard was that men are better at handling money. I believed it because that's what I heard growing up. The interesting thing is that both women and men can handle money just fine. Our society has dictated that men make the decisions, but statistics indicate that women actually excel in handling finances. We just have to let our light shine! We need to collaborate more and our light will shine even brighter.

One final myth I believed early on in life is that we can do everything on our own. This is not true. Real estate investing is truly a team sport. If we tap into our feminine skills and stop trying to do every darned thing ourselves we will be more successful.

I'm very grateful to have found a passion for real estate investing. It helped me rebuild courage to do what I do now. I can look back to 2008 when I flew to the United States with the purpose in mind to become part of a nice, big company. Understand that I did not speak English very well at that time. The company moved me to the Modesto, California, where I had to follow a lot of macho men around, trying to survive as an engineer in an engineering world run by men. Their attitude toward me was not great.

It may seem funny now to say this, but I cried every day because I didn't know what people were telling me to do. My limited understanding of English was the culprit and it would take me longer to get things done than it took other people. I look at this as my disability at that time. Like I said, sometimes everything goes back to summer camp where I worked with disabled children.

This disability, my not understanding English very well, actually gave me a path to the next step. I would learn English and take ESL classes. This opened a new channel of communication for me, but it also made me pay attention more to those around me and I was able to be a better leader. To me, life is like a jigsaw puzzle. It takes a lot of pieces (i.e., people) make this happen. The first piece is me!

I wasn't going to let my poor English skills stop me from my goals. I certainly wasn't willing to go back to Puerto Rico just because I couldn't understand what people were saying. I'm proud of myself for learning the language that allows me to speak to seasoned investors at various events. I'm proud that I can speak on stage at OCREI events. That has certainly opened a lot of new doors. When on stage I get to engage and connect with my audience. After my first time onstage it took about a week before investors had committed money to the tune of more than $1M for my projects.

When you surround yourself with the right people, those who see greatness in you that you may not see in yourself, you walk away a winner. Back when I was in a bad relationship and money was flowing in the wrong direction from my account I didn't have the right practices. I didn't even have enough money to pay my electricity. When I was first starting out in real estate I didn't know what to do, but I didn't want to go back to a job.

The funny thing is that I had become unemployable. My mindset had changed after attending women's workshops and I felt empowered. That's where I met a lot of women who would inspire me to change my life. One was Wendy Phillips, Integration Coach and Wellness Expert, who guided me through my spiritual path. Another was Deborah Razo, the founder of WREN, who saw my passion for helping women and challenged me to start the first WREN chapter in Los Angeles. Yet another was Peggy Beauregard who believed in me. These women have done a lot to help me get to my goals faster! You see, that is what networking does.

By attending networking events I gained a new perspective on real estate investing. That's where I met the developer for whom I raised capital for the first time. You better believe I tell my coaching clients to network, network, network. This brings new understanding about who we are. You see, we sometimes have to depend on other people's ideas about who we are and what we can accomplish. We have to believe them. It goes back to what I said about others seeing something in us that we may not see ourselves. That happens at networking events!

When I realized that I could never go back to a 9-to-5 job I knew there was no turning back. I would continue in real estate investing no matter what. So I kept going and kept raising private money for various projects. I heard someone say that sometimes we need to borrow someone else's confidence to build our own and accomplish our goals. Again, I am living proof.

I stayed my course even though my parents wanted me to return to a job. That was their plan because that's what they knew. But I had un-learned and saw many ways to make a living. Real estate investing tops the list.

I've gone through many adversities to get to where I am today. What I've learned is that it's less about getting over adversities than about making choices from a more empowered perspective. There is no journey worth the path if you're not consciously making choices and helping other people get to their goals.

Let's say you have to let go of a relationship. If you are focused so strongly on what it could be instead of letting go to begin anew, something healthier to your life, you will stay in that bad relationship. If we only focus on what can go wrong, we will hold ourselves back. I can give you an example for my own life.

I lost $20,000 from a man I had backed in a deal, because he lost his wife. I went too far with my compassion. I didn't have proper paperwork and I didn't do the right due diligence. For example, I unearthed a child support issues that he had not disclosed. In the end he sold the property and disappeared with the profits instead of paying me the $20,000 he owed me. That was a big lesson. Today I do my due diligence on anyone I work with and I ask myself two questions:

Will this gift me short-or long-term benefits?

Will this give life or take a life?

We have to choose our perspectives wisely. Choose to be faith-based vs. fear-based and you'll do fine. Tap into your courage. In the story about losing the $20,000 I chose to let go of negative thoughts around the money. Instead I changed my thinking and asked myself empowering questions. This is something I teach coaching clients and anyone else who will listen.

Because we tend to help others first, I've learned to ask my best version of myself what I would do for me. I know that may sound funny, but why not treat ourselves like we would treat someone else? That way we can focus on our goals.

I could have let losing the $20,000 negatively affect me, but I didn't. Adversities can take our spark away, but we cannot let that happen. We need to gather our strengths, allow time to heal and keep moving forward always.

Looking back, I realized that I took a leap of faith and I had no parachute when I went into real estate investing. I will jump again and again because when you are faith-based and you are ready to receive the blessings that come with it, somehow the universe, God, the Source or whatever you believe in conspires to bring what you need. Sometimes it might look different from what you expected, but trust me when I say it is always the right thing.

Later, I learned that my professional friends followed me in social media so they knew what I was doing. Over time they approached me to ask how they can get involved in real estate with me or on their own. That makes me really happy!

It's pretty cool when you have seasoned real estate investors calling you to help them evaluate deals. I get to create systematic approaches to help them make their best decisions and to increase their wealth through their deals. I get to be part of other investors' journeys and not just my own. Now I educate other people on how to raise capital, which is thrilling. I get to help them reach their goals. When they come back to me telling me that they raised their first few hundred thousands of dollars I actually cry! I feel like a proud mommy.

When someone asks me what I've gained from being involved in real estate investing, all I can say is that I have found a great deal of freedom. I have given over to my higher power and am on the path that makes me happiest. Real estate investing benefits my spirituality and every other aspect of my life.

Like my grandmother used to say, "Let my heart lead my focus; let my mind lead my path." That's what I've done, and I could never return to the life I once had.

I praise women I've met along the way who've influenced me to be in an influencer myself and a leader that can benefit other women's lives. I've found great joy not just in real estate investing, but because I know I am a badass at running my business! I get to tap into my mind and my heart to get to my goals. What can be better than that?

As I mentioned before, I'm a big believer in setting goals, both long- and short-term. I've already shared my short-term goals, but my long-term goals are to work with more high-performing investors. This means I'll need a bigger presence on YouTube.

I also want to expand my educational program, "The Art of Raising Capital." This has a lot to do with mindset and building relationships, so you can implement the lean process that I teach. In short my program teaches you how to become a money magnet!

Finally I want to build a few centers for veterans and the disabled. That's why I have partnered with a financial institution to help people invest in real estate smartly. This company covers all aspects of creating syndication of funds to help investors buy multifamily properties with a purpose. And that's what I am all about. I'll keep you posted on my progress. Feel free to connect with me any time and keep me accountable.

THREE TIPS:

[1] **Break the rules!** As women we are often taught that we need to follow rules, that we shouldn't speak till spoken to and that good girls seldom make history. That's bunk. I say, learn to walk on the edge and how to handle different challenges. We never know when we're going to take our last breath, so we had better define and live the life we want. If you're not doing that, why not?

[2] **Be real, not perfect!** We try to avoid mistakes and want things to be perfect. But I want you to understand it is more about perspectives. We need to let ourselves lean into the journey. We have to be true to our authentic selves. Only then will we succeed in our goals.

[3] **Learn to manage your wealth.** According to FORBES magazine, by 2030 most wealth will be in the hands of women. Best get in front of this prophecy and learn about real estate investing, so you can handle your wealth and go where you want to go. By learning to manage your wealth you can live the life that you truly want.

"I created my 60-Day Challenge program because I've seen so much inaction and so many eternal learners afraid to pull the trigger. Because I want you to do something! Not just learn."

~ Iris Veneracion, Real Estate Entrepreneur/Educator

Iris Veneracion, Real Estate Entrepreneur / Flipper & Holding Companies
Founder of real estate networking community, REInvestClub.com in Southern California

Flipping over real estate is where it all begins

If you ask Iris Veneracion, she'll tell you she is passionate about real estate because there are so many ways to make money. She'll also say she loves flipping houses because there are endless opportunities. She got into flipping at a time when there were no flipping shows on television. She had to learn by doing; she learned, like so many of us, through making mistakes and by working with other people who knew more about flipping than she did.

"I love, love, love flipping!" says Iris. "I don't care what type of house you have, all houses get old and eventually it will need fixing."

While flipping properties is near and dear to her heart, she understands that real estate investing is also a means to an end. She believes that most people that are interested in investing are ultimately seeking financial freedom. While getting fat checks from flipping is totally sexy, it is equally important to balance your investment strategies to include passive income. Her real estate investment portfolio is rich with rentals ranging from condos to single-family homes and apartments, all in Southern California. She utilizes both long and short term rental strategies. She also buys notes and creates them through private lending. As with other investors, hers has been a long and interesting journey. Here is Iris's story...

***

My journey began in 2003 while I worked in mortgage finance. It was a crazy time in the industry. Everyone was getting loans, tapping into their equity and refinancing. I remember working 12-hour days, six days a week! I was making mad money but had no life. It was during this time that an associate came to me and asked if I wanted to flip a house with her. I didn't even know what that meant. So she explained it. She had done one flip prior and messed it all up because she lived in the prop-

You GOT THIS!

erty while she was flipping it. Despite all her rookie mistakes, she still managed to break even. She was ready to do it again armed with her new found knowledge and experience. This time she wanted a partner. I couldn't resist. The market was hot and knew that if I was going to do something like this, that it would be best to do it with someone who had experience. Together, she helped me flip my first property. And, yes, we still made plenty of mistakes, but I was on my way!

That first property was a doozie. My partner gave me some criteria and I looked for the property. I looked and looked. After some time, the partner decided to take a vacation to Fiji and, of course, left to my own devices, I managed to get something under contract while she was away. I remember picking her up from the airport at LAX proudly waving the flyer of the property that I took from the open house. When she looked at it, the reaction on her face was not what I expected.

"This property looks perfect," she said, eyebrows cocked and twisted. "What are you planning to flip?"

Oh, dear...

Lesson number one: When choosing a property to flip, find one where you can add value.

Flippers look for the ugly, stinky, dirty properties that "need TLC" or that need to be updated, polished and shined! This is where you can get a good deal. The flipper's job is to find the properties that need the most help, where the sellers are motivated and where you can make a significant difference in the value of the home by the improvements you do.

The property I had was everything opposite. It was in decent condition and was practically move-in ready. I even purchased it at above asking price! I bought it all wrong, but I was not going to be deterred. Over the next few months, we rehabbed the house. We touched everything! The great thing about this first property was that I learned how to do whole lot of things... I laid tile, installed linoleum, hung kitchen cabinets, replaced hinges, put in sprinkler systems, did landscaping, painted, etc. We had a close friend of the family help us who was a retired contractor. I think he was amused that we were girls and we wanted to do all this stuff. Doing a lot of the work myself gave me an appreciation for when I would have to hire others to do that same work later. I would understand what was needed, the value of the labor, and the cost of the materials.

That experience was really beneficial!

In that first deal we made a $40,000 profit. I got really lucky. Turns out that the market was so hot that it was nearly impossible to make a mistake. Even better, we did it while working full-time jobs. Sure, it was a little crazy at times but worth it. For example, I remember racing to Home Depot after I got off work, many times making it just before they closed, to make sure we had materials for the job the next day. I was hooked! And so my addiction began… I needed my next fix.

That woman eventually became my business partner. In a very short period of time, we both quit our corporate jobs and proceeded to buy 54 rentals and flip over 150 homes together. We had a lot of fun doing it.

This leads me to Big Lesson number two: This is a business, not a hobby. Systemize and delegate!

I had read the book, Rich Dad, Poor Dad by Robert Kiyosaki. This book changed my life. I quickly realized that I didn't have an entrepreneurial bone in my body. You see, in my culture I was expected to enter the healthcare industry. Not real estate investing. Certainly not flipping properties. But after reading the book I knew I wanted to work for myself and invest. That book opened my mind! I realized that I was making the "man" a lot of money. I wanted that for myself instead. Having a partner and this insight about business gave me the courage to leave my cushy corporate job. Everyone thought I was crazy giving up a big salary with bonuses, benefits and "security" for the luxury of working for myself. Funny thing is, it didn't matter what everyone else thought. And it turned out it was the best thing I could have done. A few short years later, many of my colleagues from that corporate job were eventually laid off and the entire mortgage division was shuttered. In the meantime, I was creating my own "security" in the form of investment properties with no financial glass ceilings.

One big misconception about owning your own business is that you have a lot of time freedom. When I started working for myself I was busier than I'd ever been in my job, but I was also really happy. Many things you take for granted while working corporate, like health insurance, you soon realize, you have to pay all of it yourself!

I also had to learn about corporate compliance, and whether I should do things in an LLC or a corporation. Plus I learned that with business came corporate responsibilities, like taxes and fees, that all would land at my feet now. And I learned that as you grow you will eventually have to handle payroll. As an entrepreneur you can't call the HR department; you are HR! You aren't just responsible for your own welfare; you're responsible for the welfare of those whom you employ. I had to hire and fire everyone in my company myself. It was a pretty big learning curve, and I was lucky to have a partner and together we got through it.

As a side note, my flipping entity is an LLC that is taxed as an S Corporation. My rentals are held in LLCs and/or Trusts. Payroll is delegated to a payroll company and a book keeper and CPA versed in real estate is critical to your business. Of course, things don't happen overnight, but the faster you treat real estate investing as a business and systemize your processes, the faster it will lead you to success.

One critical thing I want to share and one of the hardest things I had to do was to learn how to delegate. There is something you can always delegate. Sometimes you feel you are the only one that can do a task, but the reality is there a many people that can do what you do, and sometimes even better. The question is are you willing to pay them and are you willing to allow them to "run with it." In other words, if you allow people the freedom to make a process their own, they may just surprise you and do it even better than you ever could. This is the power of people. This is the power of human ingenuity. You don't need to do this thing alone.

We would put our systems in place and literally leave the country to implement them. Turns out that you, the business owner, tend to be the biggest cog in the system. My partner and I loved to travel. So when we had a new system we had to implement, we would leave the country (a.k.a., take a vacation) to test our systems. If we stayed local, we would tinker too much and more than likely hold things up. There is nothing more gratifying than coming back from holiday to find out your business did even better while you were away. We found ways to make our business fun and write off our vacations!

So, first, invest time building your business. Create your systems, delegate with the right team. Scale up or scale back if you need to. Then you can create all the time freedom you want.

Big Lesson Number Three: Markets change. Goals Change. It's okay!

Since I started my business to today, I will be the first to admit my goals have changed. I began as a flipper and then quickly learned that as soon as the asset was sold, it would no longer produce income. Sure, fat checks are nice and passive income is sweet, too. There is a certain balance that can be achieved with a combination of the two. However, California was tough to cashflow at the time so I turned to out-of-state investing.

By 2005 the market was racing. I would take profit from a flip in CA and put it into properties out of state that I would buy and hold onto as rental properties. For example, I entered the Atlanta market, buying properties at auctions. It was a lot of fun. I acquired many properties quickly because I could take several properties at a time. The prices were so inexpensive compared to California that I was like a kid in a candy store... I will take three of these... and two of those... four of these. Pretty soon I found myself in several markets, including New York, Indiana, Ohio, Florida, Atlanta, Texas, Nevada and Arizona.

My goal at that time was to have 100 single-family properties. But I had bought too many too fast. I didn't have my systems in place yet, which was a mistake. However, I did spend the time to find quality property managers, and I then learned that you have to manage the managers. And apparently I was terrible at that. Without a quality system to track your rents, especially with all those properties in different areas and in several states, was a recipe for disaster.

Fast forward to 2006 through 2008 and you know what happened. I thought I bought properties that all cashflowed. But with questionable cashflow coming in, and more and more people losing jobs and not paying rent, I was headed down a deep hole, punctuated during a time when all the values were plummeting. Needless to say, it was difficult to sell real estate for profit. I lost a number of the houses I had owned. I did my best to sell the properties I could quickly, even those that were free and clear.

Losing so many properties during the downturn in the marketplace devastated me. But I knew I was not alone. That's one reason I started my club. That was in 2007. It started out as a women's club, but so many men showed up that I couldn't call it a women's club anymore. Today it is simply called InvestClub. Everyone is welcome if you want to learn about investing or do deals.

The reason for starting this club is because I wanted to create a space where investors could find help and support during that hard time. A lot of real estate investors went out of state and made mistakes. Here's one big lesson I'd like any person considering real estate investing to know. If you stop just because you get pummeled by a deal or even more than one deal, don't just stop. You can't. Otherwise you definitely lose. Real estate is a cycle just like everything else. If you stay in the game and learn from your mistakes you'll get your money back. If you apply what you learned, you will make even more!

Where there is devastation there is also opportunity. You just need to know where to look. I took all the money I had left and started finding opportunities in southern California. I was still flipping as much as I could and my eyes were open to finding properties that were under market value that would cashflow. I realized my goal had shifted. Instead of flipping everything, I wanted to keep at least one property out of every four or five that I flipped.

When I was buying out of state, I used a simple rule of thumb... the 1% rule. If the property could rent for at least 1% of the purchase price, that was a good indicator that it would cash flow. For example, if you were buying a home for $100,000, market rents should be at least $1000/month.

In 2010-11, there were opportunities in Rialto, California, for example, that you could buy for $50,000 to $75,000 each. These single-family residences would rent for $1,150 to $1,300 a month. Soon enough, these types of opportunities were showing up everywhere in Southern California. The magic I saw was that I did not have to get on a plane to visit them. Sure, the areas where you could buy these were a bit further out of Los Angeles and Orange County, but they were here in our own backyard and I could drive there to take care of issues. It was an exciting time once again.

As time passed, all my real estate wounds healed. I learned about 1031 Exchange and began trading up my properties. This strategy was great for getting rid of crappy properties in hard neighborhoods that I bought for cheap-cheap (still in California though). Using the Rialto example, after cashflowing for many years, the real estate cycle returned, the values had gone way back up again. So I would take a few of those properties, resell them at $250,000 to $275,000 each and trade up for one single-family residence in an "A Class" neighborhood in Orange County with even better cashflow.

Then I realized my goal had changed again. No longer did I want the hassle of 100 properties. At the end of the day, what was most important was the amount of passive income. My goal was now 10 to 20 properties in California, all free and clear. By trading up, I could own fewer properties that brought more income. I could make more money with one tenant in a better "hood" than with two or three out of state and with less hassle of management. Best icing on the cake? The tenant pays your mortgage off, which gets to you free and clear. Magic.

What I learned in my journey is that goals will change. Be forgiving of yourself if you change your goals. It's okay. In fact, it's natural. Markets change, lives shift. Constantly be re-evaluating your goals. Make sure you are working to your personal best which fits the needs of your life.

Big Lesson number 4: Squirrel!

Whenever I give suggestions and advice to those entering real estate investing I always let them know that there will be a lot of distractions. Also known as the shiny object syndrome, you have to be careful of it and avoid getting sucked into the many different strategies available to you. Pick the one that works best with your goals and mindset. You can try other strategies or even add on once you've established success in an area.

I know about this syndrome because it happened to me. I would go to a lot of networking events and educational events. At each they talked about something different and I would want to try it. It felt like I had a new program on my shelf every month. The reality is every strategy works if you work it. Instead, give yourself time to explore and find your niche. Expose yourself to the different niches by going to different real estate clubs that explore a variety of speakers. Inevitably, you will find something that fits your personality and will love it.

There's something for everyone. Have no money but have the time? Look into bird-dogging and wholesaling. Have a full time job and are making mad money? Consider buying notes. You like big deals? Look into commercial properties. You like fixing things and selling them? Try flipping. The more honed in you are on your focus and the more you define your goals the more successful you will be.

Find your own happy place.

No one else can define that for you.

That part is up to you, so do your research.

Don't try to compete with anybody else and certainly don't compare yourself to everyone else; this is your journey. Create what you want. Have fun. Make money. In fact, that's our club motto!

The truth is that I have found a lot of joy in my business. I count my lucky stars! I just got married and have a wonderful wife. We just had twins! I couldn't be happier.

What real estate investing has afforded me is this lifestyle, to have kids later in life, to work from my home, to have a nanny (two of them), plus I get time to actually spend with my family. Best of all I get to choose who I work with. I have a strong network of financial friends and I work with a lot of private investors who trust me and whom I trust, which is pretty awesome and critical to the success of my business! You may think this business is about properties. And the reality is, it is about the people.

Big Lesson Five: Women make great flippers!

Another thing you may have heard is that women can't flip. That's just not so. I've been flipping for a long time and I've had to learn how to communicate with men a little better. When dealing with contractors, having them bid jobs had taught me a lot. Most contractors happen to be men. Every contractor I have dealt with for the most part has a fair amount of knowledge to share. They may look it you as a woman and say, "Oh, she's just a girl. What does she know?" That's fine. You don't have to prove anything.

Just go ahead and allow yourself to be "dumb." I do not mean that you really have to be dumb, but rather let the men be the ones who answer the questions, offer suggestions. I have learned so much and have gotten far better deals that way vs. trying to be the one with all the answers. Understanding a man's mentality helps. Guys simply want to be your hero. They want to provide solutions. I learned so much more being the girl vs. being a strong competitor. Just let the guys step up. Besides, it's good for their egos.

Understand the contractor trifecta. There is Good-Fast-Cheap. Imagine a triangle with each of those qualities at the corners. Know that for the most part, you will get two of those qualities, and hardly all three. If a contractor has a good price and does quality work, the project probably won't go fast. If a contractor can do the work fast and doesn't charge a lot, the work likely will not be good. Sometimes, you will get great work done fast. More than likely you will have paid extra. There is a scenario that fits the job you are trying to fill. I find that having this awareness is helpful. In the event you do find all three qualities, praise be! Keep that contractor busy and happy.

As far as what is ahead for the future, I have been inspired to start developing. This year I will start with building Accessory Dwelling Units on several different properties we currently own. Adding a 6-unit apartment building to one of our lots in San Bernardino is also on the agenda.

Ultimately, I want to create an angel investment fund just for women. I want to gather a few of my financial friends and provide funding and guidance to the up and coming women, so that they too can participate, learn and flourish and become fearless and free.

Isn't that what life is all about? We all need to set goals, short-and long-term, and then work hard to reach them. We also need to help others reach their goals. People have helped me get to where I am today and it is a pleasure to give back.

Real estate is a great vehicle to create a life of your own design. I am grateful for the opportunities I have been given which has led to the lifestyle I love living today. It is a pleasure serving my community, my people and anyone willing to learn.

THREE TIPS:

[1] **Get educated.** Understand what you're investing in. Keep learning. Investing in a quality real estate education doesn't have to cost you an arm and a leg. Save that money and put it in a deal instead. There are great programs where not only will you learn lots, but you will also meet quality investors to build your network. I have met some great mentors that I consult with on a regular basis from simply taking their valuable class. Last, learn from people who are actually doing real estate investing, not just teaching it, and you'll do better faster.

[2] **Take action.** I mentioned earlier that I am passionate about real estate because there are so many ways to make money. Remember, all programs work. Every niche of real estate works. Yes, you too

You GOT THIS!

can make money. Overcome whatever fear you have that is holding you back and just do it. Part of the reason why I created my 60-Day Challenge, a program designed to move your forward faster, is because I've seen so much inaction. I've seen a lot of eternal learners... you know, those people who are afraid to pull the trigger? I want you to do something! Decide in your head, take the action then the results will follow. The real learning is in the doing!

[3] **Ask questions!** Don't be afraid to ask questions. Many of us don't want to ask questions for fear of looking dumb. I want to remind you there is nothing to be embarrassed about. You don't have to figure it all out on your own. Most seasoned investors I've met are always willing to help. They have a ton of experience and knowledge just brimming to come out. They are looking for people like you and me to ask the right questions. Give them the pleasure of being able to help out. It's like a gift. And believe me, there is someone out there who is doing the very thing you want to do.

BONUS TIPS:

[1] **Soar with the eagles.** Careful who you associate with. Want success and freedom? Make sure the people you hang with are there (or at least on their way). Is there an investor whose lifestyle you like? Be around them. Are there investors whose disciplines are right on the money? Learn how they do it. Jim Rohn once said you are the average of the 5 people you most hang out with. Get rid of the negative. Hang with quality people!

[2] **Flip for fast cash; hold for the freedom.** Always remember... Have fun, make money!

"Never quit and like my little fish friend Dory says, just keep swimming, no matter what! You'll get to your goals if you just keep going."

~ Kaaren Hall, CEO, uDirect IRA Services

Kaaren Hall, CEO, uDirect IRA Services

Serving others always comes first

Kaaren Hall wouldn't call herself an investor, per se. Her full-time efforts are not in fixing and flipping or hunting down real estate deals. She will tell you she has one income property that she bought with her son a few years ago. While she may not be a full-time investor she certainly helps and supports plenty of real estate investors full-time through her company, uDirect IRA Services.

"uDirect is a third-party administrator of self-directed IRA (SDIRA) accounts and we work with a trust company custodian. uDirect is focused on the customer and we just make the whole process a whole lot easier," explains Kaaren who is good at teaching others about the benefits of using one's own retirement account to invest in real estate. She is well-practiced at delivering that message. Maybe that's why she is invited to speak at events and to be a guest on so many podcasts!

Here's Kaaren's story...

***

I worked in the mortgage and real estate industries for several years and worked for two years for another self-directed IRA firm prior to opening my own shop. In my company 100% of our energies go to providing top-level customer service. We're not advisors. We don't tell you if an investment is good or bad and we don't give tax or legal advice. We don't sell anything and we're not going to recommend investments. As an educator I share the information about the benefits and rules of having an SDIRA account. Our staff helps you navigate your way through the steps of opening an account, funding it and then investing.

In addition to uDirect, I also founded "OCREIA" (the Orange County Real Estate Investors Association)in November, 2012. At OCREIA meetings people can learn various aspects of real estate investing from top professionals.

My journey to where I am today started in college as a radio announcer on campus and then in town. That surprises a lot of people. It was
something I really enjoyed. Staying in radio for a few years, I ended up
being in a radio announcer in Phoenix, Seattle, Dallas and eventually in
Hollywood. In fact, I worked on Sunset and Vine! At that time I was a
trailing spouse, following my husband around the country for his work.
All in all I put in 17 years as a radio announcer. I didn't even think about
real estate investing or doing what I do now. I didn't even think of being
in a real estate-related field. That all changed when I made friends with
a woman named Debbie who was a property manager in Seattle. Debbie
posed the question, "Why don't you become a property manager and live
on site at a property? You could do this while being on air!"

That pushed me to think of things a little bit differently. I followed
Debbie's advice and looked into getting my real estate license. After all, I
lived next to a real estate office in the building I was managing. I looked
in the newspaper and saw an ad, which said if I attended this upcoming
meeting at a local real estate office I would have a chance to win a 30-
hour class to become a real estate agent. So I went for it. The short story is
that I won the class! While I didn't know it at the time, this event set me
on a new path for the rest of my life.

I've lived in Orange County, California, for 20 years. Before I moved here
I had been working in mortgage loan servicing. That was in Dallas and in
Las Vegas. In Orange County I became involved in the loan origination
for a company at which I stayed for a few years. I learned a lot about real
estate from all sides of the deal. If something broke I learned to fix it.

Because I did well at this job I was sought by another company that is
more like uDirect. In fact, I opened the Orange County office for that
company, opening 50 accounts per quarter. That was in the beginning. By
the time I left I was opening 50 accounts per month! There was a reason
I could do so well. It's because of the large network I built in previous
years. I would collect business cards from Chamber of Commerce meetings and other networking functions until my database had over 25,000
connections. Then I developed systems for explaining self-directed IRAs
to prospects and all parties involved in a deal. Those systems were the
strength behind my future success.

Fast forward a few years and I left that company without another job in
place. What was funny was that I felt uplifted at first, but then reality hit

me and I got a little scared. It was 2009 and the market had changed a lot. By then I was a single woman with two kids to raise. I couldn't go back to radio because there are no commercial stations in the OC, but I knew how to work with SDIRA account holders. I decided to open my own company and provide the service I knew best. That was 10 years ago and it was one of the best decisions I've ever made!

At first I wasn't sure I had the skills to open and run my own company. But I proved otherwise. I learned as I moved forward. I had to stop every once in a while and remind myself that I really am the CEO of a real company. I had a lot of responsibilities and I couldn't let people down.

I've worked at several different companies and financial institutions in my life like Bank of America, Countrywide and IndyMac Bank. I knew how to apply what I learned in those businesses so I would be fine at running my own. As a Christian I believe in God and Jesus. Because of my beliefs I remind myself to have faith that everything is here for us to flourish. If you do the right things and treat people well, then your life will be good. I don't believe the uDirect was a coincidence. It was meant to be.

When I began attending real estate investing club meetings I became more active with real estate investors. I taught people how to raise capital at these meetings. I also learned more about investing. In particular I learned from a couple of people who will remain unnamed. It is unfortunate that things were not on the up and up with these two, but no one knew that then. In the aftermath, my company had 17 account holders with them and suddenly they were both up on felony charges! In short, they were raising capital from people and not doing right by them, not using their money the way they said. Unfortunately for me I was dragged into all the muck.

That was one of the biggest challenges I have been through, but with the relationships that I had developed over the years with different professionals I was able to retain a really good attorney. He was a former commissioner of The California Department of Business Oversight. When all was done and said uDirect was not implicated in any wrongdoings. We were also audited by the IRS and came away with a clean bill of health. What I learned from this ordeal was to emphasize to our account holders to check people out before working with them. Due diligence is a critical part of self-directed investing.

This was an educational experience that I never wanted to have and I never wish to repeat. I'm only sharing this so you understand that due diligence, checking people out and continuing your education are things you must do when you invest and when you are running a business. My whole reason for starting uDirect is to help people prepare for retirement, to serve people and to help them avoid making prohibited transactions with their IRAs. Every month I speak at various events all around the country in an effort to try to educate people about this important retirement tool. As a result I have spoken to tens of thousands around the country, been a guest on several podcasts and have been interviewed frequently by real estate investors who practice in different niches. All in all, it's a pretty exciting ride. To know that I'm helping people understand the power of their retirement account to invest in assets outside the Stock Market makes me happy.

That said, another WHY for doing what I do is that I can provide a good life for my kids. I can't afford to do anything off-kilter because it will affect them and, frankly, it wouldn't be the right thing to do. That means I will not work with people if I know they're unethical or if I find out they aren't doing right by others. On all sides of real estate investing and in what I do, serving other human beings is what our primary focus should be.

Whether you are a man or woman, we are all are here to serve others, and what I've found is that men and women approach business and investing differently. Men are more competitive in different ways. The women I know in real estate are more collaborative than a lot of the men I know. For example, we as women tend to believe in mentorship for the sake of mentorship. We believe in giving back. All you have to do is attend a few real estate investing events to see what I mean.

Recently I was talking to my sister Kathleen about what I've learned about real estate investing. She has always worked in corporate America. Suddenly she finds herself experiencing ageism, losing her job and having a tough time finding a new one. As a result she looked at real estate investing. We were talking in the car one day about her journey in life and in real estate. What came out of that conversation was interesting. For example, while people know a lot about real estate investing they don't always know about SDIRA rules and benefits. Even my sister didn't know how to use her retirement account as a vehicle for real estate investing. Sometimes I refer to self-directed IRAs as "the best-kept secret."

As far as SDIRAs are concerned I suggest that you get educated about what investment you are looking to do. One way you can do this is to attend events where speakers present on topics around alternative assets. At my OCREIA events in Orange County, California, you can pay as little as $20 to get in and learn from top-level presenters. That's what my sister did before getting her feet wet in investing. Next thing you know, her business partner had opened an SDIRA.

Investors are really smart people, but they don't understand everything, like all the rules and benefits around using an SDIRA. For example, did you know that 100% of the proceeds from invested funds must go back to the account? That's right. No personal use of IRA money unless you formally withdraw it from the account.

Today my sister is at an exciting part of life. She is raising private capital for future deals. Knowing that she is on a journey of learning, I gave her a few ideas. One is to attend events where at some point they will have a time that you will use to stand up and talk about your "have's or wants." This is an excellent opportunity for you to get up there and share what you really need. There will be people in the audience who can help you.

Contributing to your SDIRA is a good way to secure your financial future. As of January 2019 you can put in $6,000 a year if you are under 50 and $7,000 a year if you are 50+. This is pretty exciting stuff because it's the first time the contribution limit has been increased in five years! In 2018, you could only contribute $5,500/$6,500.

Another good thing about opening an SDIRA is that it can be tax deductible. (NOTE: I am not a tax professional and you need to seek the advice of one about your taxes.)

Did you know that there is $9.2 Trillion in IRAs in the U.S. and only about 3% invested outside the stock market? It's true. And that's kind of insane! If you are raising capital, SDIRAs are a great place to look.

Think of your IRA as a bucket. What are you going to put in that bucket?

If the IRA is with some big stock or money market and the stock market crashes, well, what will happen? If on the other hand, you were to put that money to work in real estate there's a good chance that the returns will be consistent and better than they would if you were to put them into stocks. The point is to invest in the asset classes you understand best.

Assets like real estate give you more control than mutual funds managed by someone you don't know.

While I understand all of this information and I can educate others, it is not up to my company or any of the people working for me to tell you what to do with your SDIRA funds. The account holder is in control. The question is... will you invest in Wall Street or will you invest in Main Street?

I work with a lot of seasoned investors. I've seen a lot of things over the years. I've seen some women struggle as real estate investors, but I have to say that in my profession my struggles had nothing to do with my gender. There's a myth out there that men have it easier than women or they make more money than women. This does not have to be your truth. Some women are just afraid to ask for what they're worth. That's a problem I see a lot. You have to be willing to ask for your value. You have to be willing to stand up and take charge of your situation. At least this is my experience.

uDirect had a sales person once, a woman, who had trouble asking account holders for our $50 setup fee. She felt uncomfortable, she said. She sabotaged herself. If she was going to be in a sales position and talk to account holders she couldn't hold herself back. You have to ask for the order!

That was kind of an AHA! moment for me. Maybe I hadn't realized just how women can hold themselves back by being afraid to ask for what they deserve. But that was not my first AHA! moment in life, however.

There was a time just after my divorce when I was interviewing for a job. When it came to my salary, I asked for a number bigger than I was comfortable asking for and they said yes! That really opened my eyes. In hindsight I know that what I asked for was a totally reasonable amount. I took a chance and gave them my "real number." Fortunately, the company had no problem with it and I got the job. The rest is history.

Men tend to overstate their value. Women tend to have trouble with it. We as women have to learn to ask. That's all. And then we have to learn to call in the reserves. What I mean is that once we have the high-powered job or are too busy to "do it all" it's time to hire housekeeping help and any other help we need. It's okay. We should allow ourselves that. We should always allow ourselves help and support.

I already shared a one challenge I faced in my career, which I got through it just fine. However, I didn't do it all on my own. A lot of people have helped me along the way. A lot of women have helped me. For example, when I needed seed capital and direction getting my company off the ground I was able to call on others to guide me. It was a challenge going from being an office worker to a CEO. It required a different set of skills. So I figured out what those skills were.

When you work for a company and have a boss, you can lay blame at someone else's feet and say it is the company's fault. When it's you who is the CEO of your own company it is 100% your responsibility to figure things out. When you build a team you are responsible for the members of that team. Since I didn't know everything a CEO needed to know I thought I'd better get a little help. I joined Vistage, a group that facilitated mastermind learning from other CEOs' successes and mistakes. I learned how to delegate and how to grow my network so that I could meet a lot of quality people that I could bring onto my team or to whom I could turn for answers. I'm grateful beyond grateful to have been able to learn from those CEOs.

Whenever I am facing an adversity I rely on my faith. In business, I've had to rely on my faith more than ever before. During troubled times, like the Bible quotes says, remember this too shall pass. Being the owner and CEO of your own company isn't always easy. Some days you feel alone, but we're never alone. I truly believe that. I never went to church a lot, but now the words I hear there make a whole lot more sense. Things will always get better. In business you have to deal with your competition, which brings certain challenges. But I can say that there has never been a time when things haven't worked out for the best.

In my work at uDirect, helping people is a true joy. I am happy to help people understand retirement goals and why they need to understand them. Let's take a look at the statistics.

Did you know that there are 10,000 people turning 65 years of age every day? We call this the silver tsunami. Whatever you invest in, it's really important that you look at whether alternative assets make sense for you then start by opening up and a SDIRA to make your retirement years more comfortable. If you need more proof, think about this.

If you have $100,000 in a retirement account at age 59 ½ and you take an even distribution to the age of 89, you only get $400 per month. You're not going to make it on that very well, are you? Every single one of us needs to remember to contribute to our retirement accounts and invest to build a more solid financial future. That's the kind of thing I help people understand.

Watching my staff excel in what they do also gives me joy. Watching my kids thrive because of the life I can give them through my work makes me incredibly happy. Watching my daughter graduate with a degree in math from Berkeley and teach English in Peru makes my heart soar. Watching my son become a collegiate athlete in hammer throwing, finishing 18th in the nation at nationals, makes me happy. Plus he ministers at an organization, Athletes in Action. That's amazing to me. I am really proud of my kids. To be an example for them and to provide for them makes me feel incredibly blessed.

When it comes to a long-term plan I know I will continue to educate myself and stay on this path. I like what I do. I love serving people. I will continue to serve them. And I will continue to be grateful for everything I have.

I will persevere. That's a promise. That's what I want you to do, too.

If you want success, all you have to do is wake up, suit up and show up... every day! The secret to success isn't all that difficult; you have to answer all of your calls and do a lot of follow-up. Keep in touch with people you meet and keep networking!

THREE TIPS:

[1] **Put a little money away every month to invest.** Put it in a retirement account. The best way to save is by using a retirement account where the proceeds are tax-free or tax-deferred. While I can't tell you what to invest in I can certainly tell you it's a smart move.

[2] **Network!** Your network is your net worth. That is no joke. You can't get to your goals alone. Take this seriously. By networking at events

and growing your personal network, you'll find the support and education that you need to move yourself forward.

[3] **Persevere.** Stick with it and have grit. Like Walt Disney said, "Just don't quit." Life is sure to throw you some difficulties. Don't give up. Like my favorite Pixar/Disney character Dory the fish says, "Just keep swimming!"

> "The funny thing is that I didn't set out to become a real estate investor. It really was the other way around. Real estate investing found me!"
>
> ~ Christina Suter, Ground Level Consulting / REI Advisor

Christina Suter, Ground Level Consulting / REI Advisor

A level head and good planning leads to success

For more than 30 years Christina Suter has participated in real estate investing. Today her role is more as an educator and a 1-on-1 real estate investment advisor. Christina says she loves to teach about due diligence and creative acquisitions. "I also love to review my students' investments. That way I can help them stay on track with their goals," adds Christina.

The good news is that she's an excellent educator and mentor. Her students do pretty well, which Christina says brings her a great deal of joy. After all, real estate investing is a team sport! That, says Christina, is just one of the things she learned along her journey. This is her story...

***

The funny thing about real estate is that I didn't set out to become an investor. It's not something I sought out; it really was the other way around. Real estate investing found me! In fact, it happened early in life; I started at the age of 17. That's when my mom's asthma got bad. We were living in an area where there were third-degree smog alerts. My mom had to move and I took on the role of maintaining and eventually selling her house. How that happened is that mom titled the house over to me, I rented it out to my Godparents and they bought it from me on an installment sale a few years later.

My next deal was also with family. My half-brother was stuck in a condo that he wanted to get out of. He sold it to me for the same price at which he bought it. The amazing thing is that I did the transaction even though I was only 18 years old, didn't know what I was doing and didn't know how to do everything in a deal.

Real Estate afforded me a great opportunity to help my mother. When she was ready to once again purchase a home, I was able to buy her one!

That's because my mom had been so generous as to have given me that first home to sell. I was hooked. Real estate investing was a way to create a good income. That was easy to see. What I would learn later is that there were so many ways in real estate to make money that it could make your head spin.

What appealed to me in the beginning is not becoming a professional in doing deals. It is that I would get ownership of a property if I were to buy it and then rent it out. You can say that I stumbled into real estate investing and after the first deal was done I stuck it out because it was a pretty cool way to earn a living. Plus, real estate investing is something that could work over a long period of time.

When I was young, I held a range of jobs, everything from reception-ist, working with children in childcare facilities to becoming a teacher's assistant to being a head teacher in a childcare center and then working in a marketing company and so on. All of these were low-level jobs and I thought maybe it was time to go back and earn my degree in early child-hood education. With a degree, I taught special education students and computer classes.

Even while earning my degree I stayed involved in real estate.

Fast forward to the year 2000. At that time, I was renting out a com-mercial space to spiritual teachers. It was a pretty cool place called the Ground Level Center for Living Meditation where many skills were taught, including philosophies and an awareness of the universe and en-ergies. This was on Pier Avenue in Venice, California. This place made a lot of sense for me, because in 2001 I earned my Masters in Spiritual Psy-chology degree from the University of Santa Monica. Truth is that I had started to earn a Master's Degree in Psychology at a traditional universi-ty, which taught me to heal and to understand people. I use these skills all the time in dealing with people in real estate transactions. Believe me, there is a lot of psychology that goes into communicating with all the different people that can be involved in a real estate transaction.

Something wasn't quite right. There I was running this business yet struggling with a big overhead. "I must be bad with money," I thought. But how could that be when I had more than a half-million dollars of equity in my mom's house? I needed to learn how to tap into that equity.

I got serious about taking real estate investing classes, attending networking events and doing all the things that would put me in alignment with people who knew more than I did in real estate investing. The one thing I was ready for was to participate in deals involving multifamily properties. That's about the time I started questioning whether I was in the wrong field. After all, I knew I could use my psychological training to help people no matter what field I went into. Why not go into real estate investing, something I found incredibly interesting?

In my training, I learned about the difficulty of pride of ownership, that the property should be as I would want if I lived in it and that what is really needed to serve my tenants was the three C's of real estate: clean, comfort, contemporary. So I employed these three C's in dealing with my tenants.

In 2001 made my first multifamily property purchase. It was an 18-unit building. I figured why not? I can either put money into that or into the stock market. I had no control over the stocks, plus I didn't really understand how everything worked in that market. But I surely know real estate investing! I understand that world really well. I've had hands-on experience in real estate for over a decade and it just feels natural to me. I wasn't afraid to knock on a tenant's door or to fix problems.

I kept going with multifamily property investing in Van Nuys, California, and then took two four-unit properties in Tennessee followed by a 30-unit. I did some vacation rentals and "condotels" in Hawaii, and did a little flipping in Hollywood and Los Angeles. That's just some of what I did at that time and I enjoyed every minute of it. I went from being a passive investor to being an active investor, even converting properties by doing some condo conversion projects. A lot of people do it the other way around. They go from active to passive investor.

When the market finally turned I sold several of my properties. I remember crying a lot and fighting with husband. I wanted to maintain a high FICO score and didn't want to get a job. I wanted to keep earning income from properties. I watched my properties lose value in $100,000 chunks. This made me sad, mad and scared. In the end, I sold all of my properties, some as short sales and the rest in other ways. However, that was after about six months of being emotionally frozen. It's like I couldn't take any steps or make forward motion. I sold all of my properties to minimize the stress in my life.

That's when I went into a little dark hole. Hey, I was depressed and found myself thinking that I'm a loser. I just wanted to run away. Then I thought better of my situation. I would figure out the mistakes I'd made and fix things. I remember vividly the moment when I asked myself what I would be proud of when I reached 80 years old. So, I settled on making things whole again.

My family helped me sell my properties in Hawaii and I reinvented myself as a hard money lender. I would double down on my consulting practice to bump up my income. That meant I had to figure out just how much money I had to earn to replace the income I had been earning in real estate. That was a pretty big gulp because I had been earning about $350,000 a year before the downturn!

But that's the deal in life. You have to reinvent yourself time and time again. This is especially true if you are an entrepreneur. As an entrepreneur you don't need a lot for yourself; you just need the basics. For me, all I really needed was for my daughter to be healthy and happy. Maybe this perspective comes from my being a woman. I've traveled and lived the life I wanted. I'm still living the life I want and am grateful. Things may have changed and then changed again, but I am really happy where I am now.

As women we have a tremendous capacity to reinvent ourselves. We are practical. Oddly, it is the men who are romantic. I didn't come up with that; that came from a man I know well.

As women, we are not typically the primary breadwinners. At least that's what society will tell you, but I'm a woman and I am the breadwinner of my family. My husband is older by several years, is retired and doesn't bring in as much of an income. That is okay with me. It is our agreement. I understood this going into the relationship. As a result, we have a fabulous time together. We agree that the soundness of our little family comes first. That's why I'll continue in real estate investing and private lending.

Regarding private lending, I feel like it found me. It became necessary and was easiest after the downturn of the economy at least for me with my background as a flipper and investor. One of the stand-out flips for me happened in 2017 on a house that before the downturn was only valued at about $750,000. I flipped it for a couple of million dollars! That was exciting. It showed me that everything is possible when you put your mind to it. That's something I want people who are new to real estate investing to understand. But first you have to get educated.

That's possibly the first thing a new investor has to understand. Get educated! Attend real estate investing educational and networking events at least once a week for six months. Learn from those who are actually doing deals and using different strategies so you can figure out what fits your personality and strengths. I don't advise anyone to spend $5,000 or more on a course in real estate investing until you know your focus. Once you know your focus you can place that focus in strategies that work for you.

The truth is that you can have any talents or strengths, but you won't know how they fit into real estate investing until you've exposed yourself to a bunch of other people who are doing a variety of things. Once you figure out your focus, then you can take a course. Along the way, be mindful of the shiny object syndrome that can cause you to spend too much money or make a bad investment before you are educated! Avoid the syndrome.

Ask yourself where you fit into real estate investing. Then go from there.

The next thing you can do is to network a lot.

During events and meetups you should collect as many cards as you can, like those from syndicators in the real estate investing space, people you trust and like, then follow up with them. Take them to lunch. Get to know them. Don't just let those business cards sit on your desk.

Attending events is a great way to find a mentor, too. You wouldn't believe how many people out there love to share what they know with people who are new in real estate investing. It may not cost you a thing beyond your time.

And finally to the new real estate investor or the person considering getting involved in real estate investing, think about your team. In the beginning you may be doing everything yourself. But eventually you will need a team. Who will you need on that team? Determine those players. Make a plan and build your team.

To a seasoned investor I would say just stay in your lane. Don't take on 20,000,000 things. Work with your strengths and keep building your team. Study the economy so you won't miss "the memo"! That means

You GOT THIS!

missing opportunities or missing what's happening in the market that can save you from a fall. Like when I missed the memo in 2007.

Build systems and stick to them. I am a systems person. If you build systems they will take care of your business. Part of building your systems is exposing yourself to the right people, which will minimize pain later on. Follow people like Bruce Norris and others who are very active in the real estate investing community. Email makes it pretty easy to receive people's updates and newsletters.

Staying in the know is important to all real estate investors, but it is particularly important for women in real estate investing, because we operate differently than men. We tend to share information more openly. What I see more of today is that we also celebrate our femininity more openly.

To be honest, I've never been sensitive about being a woman and the real estate world, but then people started telling me how great it was that I was a female real estate investor. That opened my eyes and I began to look around.

If you're a woman participating in deals, you have to understand that men function differently. They are more interested in the fundamentals of the deal. The function of the deal. You see, men build bridges, the stuff we use. Sure, we help. But it has always been the men who got the credit for putting the economy together. They want to build things for us women. It's just biology that they want to provide for us. That is their role, naturally speaking.

Knowing what I know about men and how they view deals, I present deals with the bottom line in mind and how the deal functions. I tell male investors about the advantages they will get from the deal and how the deal will work very specifically. As a woman you might learn to speak at that level.

We women tend to want to know how a person's family is and how they are feeling. That's how we speak to each other. Talking to other women in real estate didn't always came naturally to me. Speaking to men in real estate did. That makes sense because I was quite the Tomboy growing up!

I decided I needed to learn how to speak with all investors; not just the men in the room. So I took a workshop called PAX, which taught me how to "satisfy men celebrate women" which is their tag line, which in turn

helped me to delineate the differences in how men and women function in business and in real estate. (It also made my marriage work much better.)

When I first entered real estate investing I thought it might be what I had heard the gurus out there say... that it was a get-rich-quick thing. That couldn't be further from the truth. The real truth is that you need to get a lot of education under your belt, to get good at watching trends, and to understand exit strategies so you can get out quick if a deal isn't working out as you'd planned.

I also thought that you needed a lot of money to do deals in real estate. That's also not true, because you can start in real estate investing with nothing in your bank account and with a terrible credit score. What happens is that you'll enter the marketplace one way, continue to add to your skills and then build up. You may enter as a wholesaler and work your way up to investing in commercial properties. That is a path for many.

I also thought that I could do a lot of things on my own and make all the decisions on my own. Now I know that's incorrect thinking. Over the years I've learned to listen to opposite sides and cross-check my assumptions by seeking out the opposite points of view. That way I know I'm on the right track with my investing and my deals.

I faced a lot of challenges and different situations over my career as an investor. You can expect them from time to time. What I find is that you'll experience small challenges all the time. None of this bothers me like it used to. For example, early on I freaked out when a tenant called a health inspector on me. A tenant called because she said there were things wrong with her apartment. The inspector had to look at the whole building and not just that one single unit. The tenant stated that I had rented her a unit with torn-up carpet and baseboards. That was not the case. Her big dogs had done the damage. Even so, we fixed it on our dime. I was so worried, because it was a new situation to me and I didn't know what would happen. I let fear get to me. That would not happen today. I have more experience and I have processes and systems in place.

You'll always have problem tenants in this business. If you can't get a problem tenant out, just follow the legal process, which is there for your benefit as a landlord. Here's an example...

I had a 30-unit building in Knoxville, Tennessee, with a lot of tenant turn-over. Too much turnover. Come to find out that there was a tenant deal-ing drugs in that building. A lot of drugs. At that time, we had a female property manager. I couldn't send her in to talk to this tenant. It wouldn't be safe. So I sent a man from another property management company who was also a partner in this problem property.

The drug dealer answered the door, gun in hand. But that's not the most interesting part. He also happened to be the client of this male partner I had sent in to handle things. Due to confidentiality laws, the partner couldn't by law talk to the guy at that door. We had to find a way around that wall. We called the police. We also asked another man we worked with in a larger property management company to talk to the drug-deal-ing tenant and offer to buy him out. That way he could move before he got into more legal trouble.

This was not the only incident where drug dealing caused problems. Dealing was going on at another property, too. But it wasn't tenants. Some kids in the neighborhood were breaking into the property and do-ing deals on the grounds and breaking into cars. They broke in through a gate that had an earthquake override that they would trigger. Their activ-ities were negatively affecting tenancy. There was a 50% vacancy because people didn't want to deal with the bad element.

I came up with an easy fix. Because the drug-dealing kids were getting in through a weak point in the gate, we were able to replace the gate and fix the problem. Then we put onsite property management in place; it was a couple who were good at their job. The secret sauce was that the guy looked really, really tough. No one wanted to mess with him. The kids stopped breaking in and tenancy went back up. Problem solved.

You see, that's what you have to do as a real estate investor, especially if you own rental properties. You have to learn to bring solutions. You can't be scared. I'm certainly not. And you can't waste energy on crying. I've cried. Believe me. After dealing with all sorts of situations I have a new rule of thumb. If anybody makes me cry I hire a lawyer! If you can make me cry, you're a bigger nut than I can crack on my own. I'll bring in help.

Truth is, you will face adversities. You'll learn how to get through them or they will sink you. The way I figure it, when I am old I want to be proud of myself and what I have accomplished. I did what needed to be done.

Today, I find a lot of joy in what I do. I live by simple rules. The reason and the purpose of being involved in real estate investing is that affords me the lifestyle I want. I do it to fulfill my life's purpose and to help others reach transformation, freedom, abundance and their goals. I do the same for myself.

If something doesn't achieve these goals for me I must be doing the wrong thing. I'm proud to say that I command my freedom and make time; I want to touch people so I can help them move forward and have the same freedoms I experience. I might work every day from 9:00 to 2:00, possibly four days a week. To me that's freedom. I get to pick up my daughter from school every day at 3:00 and it fits into my schedule. If something doesn't fit into my schedule I'm not doing it. Now that's freedom!

I continue to attend and really enjoy networking events, making sure that I attend events at least once or twice a month beyond my own FIBI Real Estate Meeting. This expands my network and improves my networking skills. In the long run I want to leave a legacy for my daughter. I have the money to provide a good lifestyle now, but I also want to do more. I want to support my retirement goals. I have to raise my daughter and put her through college. Plus, I will take care of my husband at the end of his days. It is important that I give back to a man who is given so much to me over our life together and who has brought so much joy to my life every day.

My family believes in education trusts. The greatest value of an education trust is that if a parent in the family can't take care of the educational needs of his/her child the trust can! I like that idea, so I plan on creating an educational trust. After collage I want my daughter to work, because work is very important. It teaches us how to stand on our own two feet and to be responsible. Also, to be proud of what you can do and create in this world. Hopefully when she is ready to retire she can pay it forward and create an education trust for her grandchildren.

THREE TIPS:

[1] **Educate yourself early.** Know who you are as a person and an investor before you choose a niche in which to participate.

[2] Be a team player. The reason you need to know who you are in real estate investing is because it is a team sport. You need to know what you bring to the team.

[3] Know your WHY! For me it is my daughter and my legacy. Your WHY likely won't have anything to do with real estate. Your WHY will be found in personal reasons. Real estate investing can be tough. But you can make it and nothing can stop you from reaching your goals.

NOTE: Christina has a radio show called "Ask Christina First!" She also has a podcast called Real Estate Freedom Breakthrough Show available on Apple, iHeart radio, Spotify also on Amazon Fire TV and Rouku and on the Amazing Women in Radio network. Be sure to follow her adventures at the microphone.

"Terri and I are really good taking action. We discuss projects and then we move forward. That's one of the reasons we named our company Investors In Action!"

~ Alia Ott-Carter, Co-founder, Investors in Action

"Nothing gets done unless you're willing to take action and then repeat that over and over again."

~ Terri Garner, Co-founder, Investors in Action

Terri Garner and Alia Ott-Carter, Co-founders of Investors in Action

The power of complementary and powerful partnerships

Terri Garner and Alia Ott Carter set out to conquer new strategies in real estate investing together. Over the past few years that's exactly what they've done and they show no signs of slowing down. Their meeting at a real estate investing event, and subsequent 60-Day Challenge, was fortuitous. It was the business partner version of love at first sight! They knew they wanted to work together. What resulted was a solid partnership that helped these women accomplish more together than they ever could have on their own.

Even if you have investing experience, Terri recommends joining a real estate investment club. "That's where Alia and I met and forged our partnership. We've had tremendous success, because we share the same values but have skillsets that complement each other. And if skills are needed that neither one of us possess, we'll find another operational partner with those skills to help us get our projects done."

Alia agrees. "When Terri and I began working together it was kind of like magic," she says. "But the secret sauce, if you want to call it that, is when we opened ourselves to learning from others have been doing niche real estate transactions for a while. We learned more from actually doing the deals together than we ever could by taking seminars alone."

Each of these talented women had an investing life prior to meeting, but after they met and put their minds together, their goals got bigger and so did their deals. Terri and Alia absolutely rule in the space of commercial investing with a current focus on self-storage facilities where they do value-add plays to bring up the cashflow, and overall price of the property.

Let's take a look at Terri's journey into real estate investing first...

***

While I dabbled in real estate in my 30s, I didn't get serious with investing until I was in my 40s. In fact, I started my career in corporate America, working for large companies like Hughes Aircraft for six years as a mechanical engineer and for Verizon Wireless for 12 years after I got my MBA. I guess you could say I was a good corporate soldier and dutifully climbed the ranks into middle management. But, while I enjoyed my job and was making a nice six-figure salary, I knew I wasn't on the right path. What I was doing not only didn't allow me the freedom to make my own choices, but it wasn't setting me up for the retirement I wanted to have.

Like many corporate workers, the only retirement plan I had was a 401K. While I socked away the maximum 16% of my income and had company matching up to 6%, I knew that even if I built up my IRA to $1M, if I wanted to continue living a $100K/year lifestyle, or even drop to a $50K/year lifestyle, doing the math I knew I would only be able to live off my IRA for 10-20 years before I ran out of money. Then what? I'm planning to live longer than 75 or 85 years old AND really want to retire before I turn 65. I knew there had to be a better way.

For a while I dabbled in the stock market and even tried my hand at trading stock options. While I had some success, I got SO tired of the roller coaster ride of the market and hated the idea that I could lose my money overnight. I wanted something more secure. Something with brick and mortar behind it. That's when I got serious about real estate investing.

In real estate investing you don't necessarily need a formal education or a degree like I have. What was key for me was taking the skills I had learned from corporate America and applying them to my own business. My engineering background came in handy for running numbers, creating systems and being organized. My management experience helps me understand different areas of business and work with different types of people. The key is to figure out what you're good at and what you like to do, and then apply those skills to your business.

I think no matter what your background, the best way to get started, or even take your investing to the next level, is to get educated. For me, I spent $35,000 on a platinum education program that gave me 13 three-day seminars and a field training. This was a lot of money, but I had the funds from my corporate position and was able to work in the seminars on the weekends while still at my job. While I have zero regrets about spending this money since it gave me confidence and I made it back on my first fix and flip, the good news is that I don't think you have to spend the big bucks to get educated. There is so much free information out there in library books, online videos and podcasts, and information you can get in person at real estate investment clubs (many of which you can ask the organizer if you can attend the first time for free).

I always tell people to search online for clubs in your area – they are a great way to not only learn information but to meet potential partners who are more seasoned than you or who have skills in areas where you don't! Additionally, I've sold many of my early real estate books on CraigsList.com or at garage sales so check there too for some good, low-cost materials.

Regardless of how you get your education, the secret to success in investing is to take action; and then keep taking action over and over again. You're not going to change your life if you don't get moving. I've heard that only 3% to 5% of seminar attendees actually do anything with the information they learn. After spending $35K, I was committed to NOT have that be me.

So in 2006 while still at my corporate job, I started my real estate seminars and in 2007 bought two new construction rental properties, taking out a loan for each while I still had my W2 income. I still have these properties today and they bring in about $500/mo. I then took a nine-month leave of absence from my job and bought a rental property that needed to be rehabbed. Taking a leave of absence from work was a great option for me – I was able to make sure I liked working from home but still had the comfort of knowing I could go back if I had to.

Once my leave was over, I became fully committed to making the investing work. It was do or die. By now it was 2008 and the recession was starting to hit. You can imagine how my friends and family thought I was crazy!

They said, "You're leaving a six-figure job now?!"

I overheard one friend tell another, "She's going to get burned."

Oh, the nay-sayers. They were all around. But I knew in my heart of hearts that I needed to do this. I knew that if I was going to change my life, I needed to push forward. I have no regrets and the courage to take the leap is one of my proudest achievements.

At this point I was starting to run out of money and decided to try a fix and flip, so I could get a chunk of change back into my bank account. I targeted Indianapolis as my market since home prices were reasonable and it had a number of rehab opportunities due to the recession. I made arrangements with my parents to borrow from their home equity line of credit to fund the deal. (Talk about motivation!)

I was all set except one problem: I live in California and was thousands of miles away from Indiana. So I went on to Realtor.com, targeted the agents who said they worked with investors or on REOs (Real Estate Owned or foreclosed homes), and called them to narrow down my list. I had a handful of agents looking for deals for me, and the one that brought me the best deal received a commission when I bought the house and again when I sold it. My agent was my eyes and ears throughout the project and the key to my success of rehabbing remotely. I earned $40K on that deal after all expenses were paid (including my parents!) and replenished my bank account. My confidence soared.

Going hand-in-hand with rehabbing, I decided to expand my training by learning how to stage a home to make it sell faster and for a higher price. If there was something I didn't want a repair I could just "stage" around it so it didn't stand out. If there was a scar on a counter top I could put candles over it. If there was a bad spot in the carpet I covered it with a throw rug. Of course you have to disclose everything before closing but staging definitely helps with a first impression.

I enjoyed the staging and saw an opportunity to run two related businesses side by side – rehabbing and staging. I became a certified stager and went into business with my mother. For two years we were very successful, but staging was very laborious and didn't bring in the chunks of change that rehabbing could. I soon realized it was a diversion from doing bigger real estate deals. So we closed down the business and I turned back to rehabbing.

While I'm grateful for the staging experience, in hindsight I wish I had just kept going with fixing and flipping, or fixing and renting out properties. My lesson learned? Don't be distracted by bright shiny objects. It's very difficult to operate two businesses at the same time, even when they are somewhat related. Find the strategy that works for you and focus, focus, focus.

Around this time I met Alia at a local investment club (Iris Veneracion's InvestClub – love it!) and we began working together in early 2010. From the beginning we could tell our personalities complemented each other's. Alia is more of a creative person; I love spreadsheets. Our first project together was a flip where we pooled our resources to get it done. Let me tell you, while I was comfortable working alone from home, it was really nice to have someone to bounce ideas off of, someone to commiserate with when things go wrong and celebrate with when they go right.

In addition to rehabbing, Alia and I started lending on other people's rehabs. In other words, we would raise the money, and then loan it to rehabbers who did the work. In effect, we were the bank that was creating performing notes. Then we decided that since performing notes were going so well, why don't we get into non-performing notes too. (This is where you buy notes that are in default and work them out with the home owner.) I guess you could say we were adding to our skill sets and figuring out what we liked and didn't like in each strategy. However, remember what I said about bright shiny objects and starting a side business? Non-performing notes is a whole different beast from performing notes and I soon realized I had created myself another job! My lesson learned, again for a second time: Don't be distracted by bright shiny objects. Focus.

Another lesson driven home from this period of trying different strategies is that if my end goal is to retire, I needed to find a strategy which generates passive income (where you receive cashflow without spending much of your own time) versus active income (where you trade time for dollars, a.k.a., a job!). My plan from the beginning had been to fix and flip a property (active income) then use the profits to buy a rental property (passive income) and repeat this process to build a portfolio of rental homes. While still a great strategy (my husband and I have kept five of our single-family rentals; one of which is a vacation rental), now I'm much more interested in owning larger commercial properties which put out more cashflow and have a larger growth potential. ("Commercial" properties include apartments with five or more units, mobile home parks, storage facilities, retail/office space, billboards, etc., and "residential" properties include one- to four-unit residences.)

You GOT THIS!

With single-family rental properties, when someone moves out you lose cashflow immediately. Typically, you need to repaint and do repairs before you can get another tenant in. With commercial properties when one tenant moves out, you still have multiple other tenants paying rent. You don't have that sinking feeling of your cashflow dropping. For Alia and me, once our confidence grew, we shifted from lending and working on single family residences and are now focused on lending and buying self-storage facilities.

Why self-storage facilities? In self-storage, you are not dealing with live-in tenants; you are dealing with storage units rented by tenants who rarely visit the property. It's four walls and a roll up door. One tenant moves out, you broom sweep the floor and you're ready for the next tenant to move in. No toilets to burst in the middle of the night. Also, since no one is living in the units, the Fair Housing Laws don't apply and it's much easier to get rid of a tenant if they keep missing their monthly payments. Each state has a process for the units to be emptied out and the contents auctioned off, typically within 30-45 days. It's a lot easier than dealing with tenants who have squatters rights and refuse to move out, causing a much lengthier eviction process

Regardless of which investing strategies I've done in the past, building a team has been key to my success. No matter what you're doing as an investor, you can't do everything on your own. If you want to grow your portfolio and your cashflow, you're going to need a team. When Alia and I decided to move into the commercial arena, we first found somebody to work with who was familiar with self-storage; his name is Al and he'd already done a number of deals in this space. Since Alia and I had several years' experience as private lenders under our belt, we brought in the investors and Al headed up operations. We formed a partnership with each of us as co-owners of the property. Since 2014, we've acquired 13 storage facilities and are still counting.

Like a lot of people in real estate investing, I have both short-and long-term goals. My first shorter-term goal is to finish out my portfolio with more storage facilities and get to my magic monthly cashflow target. Beyond that I want to diversify. There is diversity in location, so I want to have properties in different areas of the country and world. To keep all your properties in the same area isn't a good idea. Can you imagine if you do and a hurricane or tornado comes through, wiping them all out at once? Diversification equals a good retirement and asset protection.

I love real estate investing, but it's also a means to an end. As I've said a few times, I'm looking to create a great retirement and a lot more time freedom. I also happen to have a passion for the environment, so I want to get more involved in charities that pertain to bettering our environment and creating a better world to live in. Right now I live in Fallbrook, California, a beautiful area and I want to keep it that way so I do a lot of volunteering in my community.

I don't plan to ever completely walk away for real estate investing, just perhaps reduce the time I spend on it. As a real estate investor your personal and professional life can flow seamlessly together. You have freedom to choose how you spend your time. To me, that is the definition of success: Doing what you want, when you want, with whom you want it. You can't find that in the land of cubicles and bosses. When I became a real estate investor I never looked back. I am living my ideal life.

If you're new to real estate investing, get educated. I don't care what that looks like or where you get the education or who will you work with to get that education, just get educated about the different strategies you can use in real estate investing to make both active and passive income. There's no one right way to approach the business. All strategies are viable, and there are plenty of sub-niches. Learn a couple of strategies and focus on the one that appeals to you the most and fits your overall goals. Then take action, focus, don't get distracted and just keep going.

If you're a seasoned investor there are a few things you can do to up your game. I strongly recommend setting up repeatable systems. This will help to simplify your business and keep it organized. Then create teams that can scale with you as your grow. If you are ready to move to the next level, find a partner or partners who have complementary skill sets but with the same shared values. That way, when things go bad, you can approach things together. If you can approach them in the same way with the same attitude like Alia and I do everything turns out well. We love working together. It's a great partnership and I look forward to seeing what else we will achieve together!

THREE TIPS:

[1] **Know your WHY!** Why are you participating in real estate investing? Why are you interested in taking this crazy journey?

You GOT THIS!

There'll be falls along the way. I guarantee it. You will have failure events, too. You need to "Fail Forward." Keep going. Knowing your WHY will help you keep going when you fall. It has to be a personal WHY, too. It can't just be "to make a dollar." Yes, you want to make money, but why do you want to make that money? You want to make that money so you can _____. That's something that you have to decide for yourself. And it must resonate with you personally. Your WHY will pull you up by the bootstraps and help you ride out the tough times.

Whenever I face adversity I focus on my end goal. I want a good retirement and to have a good, quality of life. Having a clear end goal and understanding that it's not necessarily a straight path to success... it will zigzag this way and that way. But you have to keep going forward. Knowing your WHY will help keep you motivated.

[2] Get things in writing. This may seem obvious but it's worth stating. Real estate investing is a business and you must utilize contracts that clearly state what is expected to happen and what the consequences are if they don't. You should never give something unless you get cash, or a contract, in return. If you're selling a property, don't hand over the keys until you have the money or contract in hand. If you're hiring a contractor, have the contract signed by both parties before sending any funds. If you're renting, have the tenant sign a contract before they move in. Also, depending on the situation, you may want to use a notary. They are inexpensive and provide proof of date and signature. As one of my past mentors used to say, "In God we trust; everyone else puts it in writing." I couldn't agree more.

[3] Set up processes and a team (or teams) so that they win when you win. That's what was needed when I did my out-of-state rehabs. I found a real estate agent who had a vested interest in having my rehab go well (so that he can also sell the property once the flip was ready to go). I only needed to go out one time to look of the property prior to buying it. Everything else, including the entire rehab, was handled from my desk and my phone. I was able to go to my local Home Depot or Lowes in California to select a product, buy it, and then have my contractor pick it up in Indiana. Because the real estate agent was checking in on the property regularly and sending photos back to me, I knew things were being done correctly and the project went smoothly and made a nice profit for all of my team members.

A team also includes having a partner, which is a great way to help share the burden and keep you uplifted in your business. Find partners with complementary skill sets and clearly define each of your rolls. Alia is a go-getter and a great networker. She loves getting out there and talking to people. I enjoy doing the numbers and, oh, those beautiful spreadsheets.

Keep in mind that a partnership is only as strong as the group's weakest link, meaning you have to be as concerned about your partners' success and happiness as you are about your own. All partners need to win in order for your business to work. Choose partners that have the same values as you do and who approach the business with a similar integrity and concern. Once you find that right dynamic, you will be unstoppable!

Now that we've heard Terri's tale, it's time to learn of her stellar partner Alia's journey...

Like Terri, I had a little bit of an advantage regarding a basic understanding of real estate from an early age. As a kid, I essentially grew up with a paintbrush in my hand and a woodshop in my basement! My parents had some involvement in real estate investing and I had my hands in a variety of house projects for as long as I can remember. My parents owned a property in Hawaii, and our vacations to the island often included trips to the hardware store, plumbing repairs and cleaning up the condo for the next tenant. I also enjoyed looking at open houses and vacation rentals with my mom as a teenager and always knew that real estate would be part of my life, but didn't imagine how significant it would become.

My first foray into real estate investing started in the late 1990s. At the time, I was working for a non-profit organization called Network for Good. While I loved doing meaningful charity work, I knew that if I were to remain an employee, the income would never allow me to have the kind of lifestyle or freedom I desired. My philosophy was that if I was able to build wealth and achieve financial freedom – I could do even more good with my time and money. As luck would have it, I had just read the book by Robert Kiyosaki, Rich Dad Poor Dad, and started taking real estate classes.

Not too long after that, I bought a home in Mission Viejo, California, where I planned to live for two years, make some improvements and then sell the property for a profit with the homeowner capital gains exemption. What happened was a slightly different story. Instead of doing a small remodel, I ended up tearing half the house down and adding an 850-square-foot addition, all while getting my hands dirty doing part of the rehab. I used to joke around that date night started on Friday with a trip to the landfill and would end up coming home with a trailer full of supplies from Home Depot. Once the addition was complete, it looked so nice that I ended up remodeling the rest of the house to match it. I didn't sell it in two years like I had planned either; I held onto it for 14 years – all the way through the recession and start of the recovery, renting rooms to roommates while I lived there and entire families when I didn't. During that period, I bought a couple of single-family homes, a triplex and began my commercial investing. All in all, I was doing well enough to eventually leave the day job and still survive.

In 2008, as we all know, the bottom of the market dropped out. I saw what was happening because I watched the trends and I had been attending seminars and club meetings. In other words, I saw the opportunity on the horizon, and wanted to be prepared with knowledge to seize it. One of the best things that happened is that I met Terri Garner, my perfect partner, my first day of attending Iris Veneracion's InvestClub for Women and together we joined her amazing 60-Day Challenge. And a challenge it was!

During those 60 days, I had my feet to the flame, learning what it takes to be successful in real estate investing and finding, negotiating and acquiring great residential deals. Attending investment club meetings was a great networking opportunity; attending made me realize I wasn't alone and that I could find partners to work with.

Soon after the challenge, Terri and I began lending, and eventually investing in performing and non-performing notes. The hard money lending was a wonderful way to make easy, predictable passive income. For about four years straight, our batting average of doing good deals with great borrowers was impeccable.

The portfolio of non-performing notes we bought were a little more like a box of chocolate-covered surprises – you could see some detail from the initial analysis, but you never know what you're truly going to run into, until you own the paper and start dealing with a delinquent borrower. Our success with non-performing notes was a mixed bag of singles, strike outs and a few home runs. I enjoyed analyzing the deals prior to purchase but, as Terri mentioned, she and our other partner who were in charge of getting borrowers to make payments again created themselves a debt collection job.

At one point in the midst of my lending career, I was presented with an opportunity to purchase a heavily discounted mobile home park, with an extremely short timeline to close. I ended up buying the park with a group of guys – most of whom I hardly knew. There were moments of insanity, but based on the numbers, I knew we could screw this up many ways and still do great with it. While the numbers on this property did turn out to be an amazing deal, it wasn't without its challenges and gave me one heck of a learning curve… especially on the topic of partnerships.

Several valuable things came out of that deal; the first was confidence… If I could deal with all the things I had to do on this property, I was pretty certain I could do just about any kind of commercial deal. Over the course of five years, I dealt with changing partnership structures, rehabbed over 50 homes, had our main water line go out, worked through tenant disputes and of course, plus the occasional drug bust and house on fire. The cashflow on this property was solid from day one and just got better as we improved the park. I was also grateful to have an experienced on site property manager who taught me a lot about owning this type of asset, but I must say, mobile home parks are anything but passive.

It was also through this deal that I met our self-storage operational partner, Al. I got to admire his strength of maintaining a logical, level head throughout challenging situations. He was also very pragmatic about getting things done and earned my trust.

By owning a mobile home park, with multiple park owned homes and many units of cashflow, I was able to create teams, repeatable systems and infrastructure, which would later come in handy when we began to expand our self-storage portfolio.

Going back to the lending side of life, which was my primary business at that time, Terri and I eventually broke our perfect streak of lending deals in 2014, when we had a borrower default on us with two lending deals in Palm Springs. Because of our experience with nonperforming notes and dealing with foreclosures, we kind of turned this experience into a game. We went to the courthouse steps to witness the foreclosure (hoping someone would bid up the deal and take it off our hands). While that did not occur, we ended up finishing the rehab, beautifully staged the properties and sold them, all while keeping investors current with their payments.

We decided after coming out of pocket on those two deals, we wanted more stability and cashflow, with less risk. We were already a few years into a market recovery and wanted to position our portfolio for long-term, recession-resistant cashflow. It was no more than a few days following that conversation when Al (my partner in the mobile home park) asked us to fund one of his self-storage deals. Everything about it made sense, so we said YES and have continued to invest with Al as our self-storage operational partner ever since.

Today Terri, Al and I continue to buy underperforming self-storage facilities, ensure that they are properly marketed online, have good signage, quality management and do other value-add plays to bump up their value. In doing so, it helps the property earn more cashflow over the long term.

I won't go into too many details here, because Terri covered this part of our journey already, but if you want to download a great eBook on how to do what we do in self-storage, you can do so at www.investorsinaction.com. Browse the articles while you're there, because they are there to help you.

If you are new to real estate investing or looking to up your game, you should never stop reading articles and books on all the different strategies. It's just smart.

When working with any person who is new to real estate investing I start by asking a couple of simple questions:

1. What are your financial goals? Is it cashflow, quick capital gains or something else that you're after?

2. What are you great at doing and what are the things you DON'T love doing?

Then we work backward from those goals to the steps that you need to take to get where you want to be. Not every strategy is good for every investor. And not every role within an investment company is the right one for you. It's good to define a niche that fits your personality and then focus on that before trying another strategy.

As an example, while I started out with single-family residences I did not stay in that space. I wanted to do commercial properties because, and you may not believe this until you actually try one, they are actually easier to manage. That's because you have enough income from the bigger properties to hire a good manager to oversee operations and handle issues. When you purchase single family residences, especially if they are within driving distance, people tend to take on the property management role themselves, which can be time-consuming and stressful.

No matter what area of real estate you might be interested in you should:

1. **Assess your goals** – I cannot stress this enough.

2. **Figure out what resources you have and what your financial capability is so that you can actually get to your goals.** A good rule of thumb is asking how much you need to survive, because the "extra" can go into your investment funds. Try to keep your FICO score up, because you may need to get a loan from the bank for your first couple of properties.

3. **Know thyself** - Figure out your strongest skill sets and personality traits. For me, I love connecting with people. I like helping them find properties; discuss deals and get juiced by helping people succeed in real estate. Because I am a creative, people-oriented, big-picture type of person, I don't typically like to spend time immersing myself in paperwork and other minutia.

4. **Find the right people to collaborate with, whether that's partners, employees, service providers, construction people or anyone else you'll need to get a project done.** You'll want all of the puzzle pieces to fit together. Thank God for Terri and Al. Terri LOVES her spreadsheets, and is incredibly well organized in dealing with the details. Al is great at managing tough situations and keeping a steady pace of improvements going on each property. Wealth Dynamics offers a test to define your best profile – and, more importantly, the best profiles to partner with.

If you're more of a seasoned investor, the same rules apply. You're definitely going to need to assess your goals and skills, but your experience will be based on what you did and did not like about what you've already been doing in real estate. You'll let your experiences take you to the next level. That means you must continue to get educated and surround yourself with people are doing bigger deals than you and who are playing at a higher level than you. Do not be afraid of being a part of a group where others know more than you. I love masterminding with other smart investors. There is no better way to learn. It's a great way to find mentors, too!

The truth is that you'll keep getting educated no matter when you join like-minded groups that hold you accountable for taking action and playing a bigger game. I still do this. In fact, I just recently joined a deal exchange group. There are many clubs and in-person groups, but you shouldn't stop there. You should also join online groups and build relationships with people everywhere you can. As your network grows, so does your net worth. Resources like Bigger Pockets host a ton of valuable education and message boards.

There is a mental barrier that some women have – which is that the ladies have a harder time succeeding in real estate than men. Thankfully, it's not just the ol' boys club any longer. While some of that attitude still exists, I find that for women who are willing to shine, there are often unique opportunities to step into the spotlight and get recognized for what they are doing because they are women. Even when you're in a male-dominated niche, as a woman you can do just fine. All you need is the confidence to walk into any room at any networking or educational event and start talking to people.

I remember one time when Terri, Al and I walked into a room at a real estate event filled predominately with older gentleman who were commercial lenders and brokers. That sure didn't match the look and feel of our diverse little troupe… we essentially checked all the boxes of a "minority-, veteran-, women-owned business." You might think that would've intimidated us and that people wouldn't want to talk to us. But because we were different, we garnered more attention than the other people in the room, almost like we were a magnet for them. These other attendees were curiously drawn to us, which opened up a lot of conversations. We walked away from that event with a lot of new contacts and funding partners.

The challenge I've occasionally had as a woman, especially with older investors or subcontractors, is the assumption that I must know very little about investing or construction. I often take people by surprise when I list some of the types of projects that I've done or that I manage a syndicated fund. I've had people attempt to take advantage of me (contractors, in particular), but I've learned to stand my ground and demonstrate that I have an understanding of their area of expertise as well. I find that asking a lot of questions and openly sharing my experience always helps.

When it comes to doing business, it doesn't matter if you're a man or a woman, if someone is out there doing deals successfully, so can you! Just get good at seeking mentors to fast-track your path in getting where you want to go.

The funny thing is that I never saw myself as a commercial real estate investor. But that's only because I didn't know how to think big. Now I think big. Really big! The concept of owning commercial property is no longer a foreign idea or scary thought in my mind. They say once you expand your comfort zone, you can't go back to the way things were before. It's not to say that investing in commercial is without challenges – there will always be ups and downs, no matter what you do.

Terri and I together, and separately, have certainly experienced our share of challenges. But we never hesitate in doing what is right and taking care of what needs to be done. As I shared earlier, we had those two loans that defaulted where we had to step in and take control of the property. In the end, we lost money on those deals, because we had to keep our investors paid. The truth is that we could've left the investors hanging, but we would never do that. I know how it feels to be short-changed by an investor that I put my trust in, and I never want to be that person. Through that challenge we strengthened the trust with our investors because they had greater confidence in our ability to do the right thing, when things get hard.

The terrific thing about that ordeal was that Terri had the same mindset about what we should do – without hesitating we both rolled up our sleeves and took care of it. There is no better way to test a partnership than being thrown a difficult situation and seeing how the other person handles it. I'll stick with Terri Garner for a long time to come. We do well together and complement each other's strengths.

You GOT THIS!

I cannot stress enough that when it comes to partnerships you have to see eye to eye with your partners. If it's not working between you, call a spade a spade and end the partnership, which usually entails selling the property, buying someone out or going through the courts. You have to be willing to do that, because staying in a bad partnership can cause a certain level of insanity. I'll tell you, it was a really long stretch with my mobile home park deal, but I eventually got to the end zone with that too.

Another major lesson I learned from investing is to not get stuck sitting in the "wrong seat on the bus." What I mean by that is, don't take on roles or activities that you're not aligned with, because you might be in for a really long ride. Stay within your lane of strengths and choose partners whose strengths complement yours. It's not fun when you have to take over other people's jobs to get things done, but you sometimes have to do that if the people you rely on fall short of their commitments.

Throughout the years, I got good at saying no – no to working with people who aren't a good fit. No to potential people who dangle money in front of me, but who have questionable ethics. No to deals that don't fit my niche. When you're really clear on your values, your goals and the specifics of how you want a deal to be structured, it becomes MUCH easier to say no to the wrong partners, investors, associates, sellers and buyers. By educating yourself and surrounding yourself with people from whom you can learn, it empowers you.

If someone were to ask me what keeps me going I would say it is my desire to create freedom and a positive impact on the planet! Real estate investing plays a huge role in my goals, because it affords me the financial stability to create a life I really want and spend quality time with my family.

I get to experience new things through real estate investing, too, which excites me. Time freedom creates a lot of joy in my heart, because I get to schedule my life around my own goals and projects. I don't have to function within the confines of a 9-to-5 job. I don't have to answer to a boss. I don't have to work in a cubicle.

Like Terri, I have a couple of long-term goals. I want to get bigger, more creative deals in my portfolio of properties, especially in the commercial arena. I'd like to help my husband retire from his 9-to-5 grind and through my investing efforts I'll get to spend more time with our kids. That's been very important to me for a long time. In fact, that is my biggest WHY in creating financial freedom – so I have more time and ability to spend with my loved ones.

I look forward to what the future holds even if I'm not sure what that looks like quite yet. I am working as an advisor to my husband's Virtual Reality company and I'm actively helping our team (and others) find some great investment properties. I'll keep working with my business partners for years to come as most of my strategies are long term "buy and hold" investments for retirement cashflow.

THREE TIPS:

[1] **Partner smart!** You want a partner with those whose skills that complement your own. You may want to start by partnering with a mentor who can help you see the big picture, because that person may be able to see your strengths and path more clearly than you can.

[2] **Get a mentor or two.** Surround yourself with people who are way more seasoned then you in real estate investing. In fact, surround yourself with people who do a whole bunch of different things in real estate so you can choose the strategies that fit your personality best.

[3] **Put fears aside.** Even if you're afraid of doing a deal or trying a new strategy, do it anyway. But be prepared. Fear often shows up right when you're getting ready to try something new. Let it be a good motivator. Don't let it roll you into a ball and paralyze you. Do your research and then take action. Whether a deal goes well are not, at the end of the day you're going to learn new things. Wouldn't it be better to say you took action, tried new things and failed rather than that you did nothing? Besides, the lessons you learn when making mistakes in a deal or a project may be the exact thing that gets you over the next hurdle in your journey and in future deals.

"My innate feminine desire to nurture, love and teach is ignited when I get to add value to all of the lives I touch."

~ Jennie Steed, Wealth Strategist and Financial Educator

Jennie Steed – Wealth Strategist & Financial Educator, Paradigm Life

Wealth Strategist & Financial Educator

Jennie Steed teaches others about the principles of financial freedom and accountability, also known as the "Perpetual Wealth Strategy." She explains that true financial freedom comes with the application of the 7 Principles of Prosperity* along with a deep understanding of the hierarchy of wealth. Teaching these principles is something Jennie is passionate about, because it's a way for her to serve others in moving ahead and achieving their goals with greater clarity and efficiency.

"Wealth-building begins with education first. I cannot stress the importance of educating yourself. It's your stewardship. Without it, it is gambling, which is how most of people invest. The principles of financial freedom and accountability are vital," says Jennie, "then making sure that your foundation is solid by maximizing control and minimizing risk. What most don't understand is with increased risk, comes a loss of an element of control, so only take on additional risk if you're forced to do so, such as time restraints or other similar restraints, and only if you are confident in your understanding of the investment. I love teaching people how to have their money performing multiple jobs at the same time. In other words, making sure it is adding value to your life in more than one way, and working for you simultaneously in 2+ areas. If there's something I know to be true, it's that four of the greatest attributes of owning real estate are its ability to create cash flow, to use leverage, gain tax benefits, all while continuing to appreciate in value. The Perpetual Wealth Strategy has those same attributes and more. When we combine real estate investing with the Perpetual Wealth Strategy, we can create velocity, creating increased efficiency and wealth creation more so than with RE investing alone."

Like I said, Jennie is an educator, but she wasn't always. Here's her story...

***

I became a client of Paradigm Life in 2010 after learning and applying the principles of financial freedom and accountability this group teaches. What this did was add peace of mind to my life in ways I could have never imagined. In 2013, I decided that being a Wealth Strategist is what I wanted to do, which is to bring about the same peace of mind I now enjoy into other people's lives. I am so grateful to Patrick Donohoe for seeing my passion and for bringing me on to join his team of Wealth Strategists. Since 2013, I have had the privilege of working with hundreds of families, in all walks of life, to align their finances, in order for them to achieve financial freedom.

My work is my passion, and some of these staggering statistics led me to being so passionate about helping assisting others in creating and maintaining financial stability and true freedom:

- According to the US Census Bureau, out of about 12 million single parent families in 2014, more than 80% were headed by single mothers.

- If a single mother is able to work, her earning power still lags significantly compared with men's, about 68¢- 78¢ to a $1 for the same job — leaving a wage gap of 23¢ to 32¢ on the dollar.

- According to economist Evelyn Murphy, president of the WAGE project, the wage gap costs the average American full-time woman worker between $700,000 and $2 Million over the course of her lifetime.

- The US Department of Agriculture revealed that to raise a child born in 2013 to the age of 18, it will cost a middle income earner just over $245,000, that's up 2% from the year before. This is NOT including the cost of college.

- The average cost of tuition and fees for the 2014–2015 school year was $31,231 at private colleges, $9,139 for state residents at public colleges, and $22,958 for out-of-state residents attending public universities.

- Depending on the study, and there is a large variance in quoted statistics, but approximately 50% of marriages end in divorce. Depending on how often MONEY is the source of the arguments, as high as 81% of divorces are money related.

- According to Forbes: The number of wealthy women in the US is growing twice as fast as the number of wealthy men. Currently, 45% of American millionaires are women, and some estimate that by 2030, women will control as much as 2/3 of the nation's wealth.

- According to the Social Security Administration: 80% of men die married, while 80% of women die single.

- Half of women over age 65 outlive their husbands by 15 years

- Seven out of 10 currently married American women will become widows at an average age of 59.

Why are these statistics so staggering?

Honestly, I feel that it is because women tend to undervalue their worth and what they contribute. I also feel that a lot of the time when women enter the workplace, they are under a false notion that they get to create value the same way that men do. That is primarily because, especially in finance, investing is inherently masculine. This is not a bad thing, but it is something that should be evaluated more closely.

Maybe it really is true that Men "Masculine" are from Mars and Women "Feminine" are from Venus. Perhaps this is the basic reason for the staggering statistics. Men and women are truly different, especially in how they conduct business. This is good news. We always have the yin/yang.

That said, neither male nor female is better or worse than the other, just different. Some of us, not necessarily gender-specific, have a dominant and prevailing energy base and can often switch back and forth between the two. Take a look at this:

Masculine	Feminine
Decisions based on Facts	Decisions based on Emotion
Fix the issue right now/get to the bottom line	Process emotions/like to talk about/process
Immediate/nearsighted focus on objective	Big-picture/ farsighted focus on objective
Consistent emotional pattern	Fluctuating Emotional pattern

Understanding and honoring the differences is what will bring about the most fruit. We shouldn't try to be something we are not. Remember that both the masculine and feminine each has their own unique contribution to the overall success of any financial plan. When we understand the value that we each bring, we can complement each other to create massive results. Having a deep understanding of the differences in how a man's mind functions differently than a woman's guides me in assisting the INDIVIDUAL in front of me.

Here's where I can step in and work with people to get them moving on the right track. I meet one-on-one with every client and get a clear picture of their WHY. We can then work together as a team to understand their goals and timeline, which will ultimately provide an outline to how I can assist them in getting from where they currently are, to where they want to be, and in the most efficient way possible.

We will also take a look at their financial foundation, to see if there are any holes or cracks that could undermine their achieving their goals. Most of the people I talk to are concerned with 1 or 2 things – growing their assets and income streams, and/or protecting their assets and income streams. The biggest problems I find exist at the foundation on which their assets and income streams are built upon. This is a huge problem. The longer the problems go unaddressed, the more catastrophic the loss or outcome. As you know, identifying underlying problems, as early as possible is vital for success, especially in real estate investing.

As there is a hierarchy of needs, and a hierarchy to many other aspects of life, there is also a hierarchy of investing. A properly structured hierarchy of wealth, which begins with a solid, stable foundation. Successful real estate investors understand this hierarchy of wealth, and only build up, if the foundation is solid and stable, and can handle the additional load. If the foundation simply needs to be expanded, I assist in getting it expanded. If there is no foundation, I assist in getting that set up. If there are holes or cracks, I assist in getting those repaired first, then get onto the growing your wealth to its max potential. At that point, we can proceed with peace of mind, knowing that everything is growing and protected.

If I can change some of those staggering statistics I shared above, all the better!

In what I do I get to add value to people's lives and I love it! It is my intention to continue in my role as a Wealth Strategist with Paradigm Life.

One group of people I help happen to be real estate investors. Literally, it brings my heart joy.

Those new to real estate investing tend to have a lot of fear about taking their first steps and making deals. I see this sometimes. If I could give them a bit of advice it would be to make sure that they treat themselves as their number-one asset ALWAYS! You are the machine that is driving you closer and closer to your dreams, your goals and the life you want to live. Embrace your unique self. When you do, you will experience all the abundance you seek.

The very first step to creating financial freedom is to know your VALUE. This is vital in order to create your strategy. When planning for anything, be it short-term or long-term, you must begin with a solid foundation on which you will build your future. That foundation must follow the 7 Principles of Prosperity to support those building blocks. I recommend following the 7 Principles of Prosperity to every aspect of your business, dealings and negotiations.

If you've never heard of the 7 Principles of Prosperity, it is trademarked by Prosperity Peaks' Kim Butler, who also happens to be a friend and mentor. She couldn't be happier that I am sharing these with you!

Here are the 7 Principles of Prosperity I spoke about at the first of the chapter:

1. **THINK** – Owning a prosperity mind-set eliminates poverty; scarcity thinking keeps you stuck.

2. **SEE** – Increase your prosperity by adopting a macro-economic point of view—a perspective in which you can see how each one of your economic decisions affects all the others. Avoid micro-economic "tunnel vision."

3. **MEASURE** – Awareness and measurement of opportunity costs enables you to recover them. Ignore this at your peril

4. **FLOW** – The true measure of prosperity is cash-flow. Don't focus on net worth alone.

5. **CONTROL** – Those with the gold make the rules; stay in control of your money rather than relinquishing control to others.

6. **MOVE** – The velocity of money is the movement of dollars through assets. Movement accelerates prosperity; accumulation slows it down. Put money to use.

7. **MULTIPLY** – Prosperity comes readily when your money "multiplies"—meaning that one dollar does many jobs. Your money is disabled when each dollar performs only one or two jobs.

Sometimes I meet seasoned investors who simply don't have a safe, guaranteed place to store cash as it awaits the next job. With the Perpetual Wealth Strategy, I get to provide a way protect and grow your money, so as to not leave it lazily sitting idle between jobs.

You must remember that your money always needs to be moving, because movement accelerates your prosperity. Peace of mind comes from the ability to be crystal clear on the investment decision before making a move. I see too many times where an investment is chosen just so the money isn't sitting in the bank doing nothing, which adds risks and a loss of control. This is not a habit of the wealthy. If we can remove that knee-jerk reaction from the equation, we can educate first and then act, knowing that the money is protected and growing at the same time, thus bringing about less risk and more control.

This brings me to something I learned over time about risks and rewards. A myth really. I had always heard that taking on additional risk means there will be an additional reward. That couldn't be further from the truth, as taking on additional risk actually means increasing your likelihood of loss.

Growing up and in my young adult life, I was taught that the key to making massive amounts of money was to take on risk, so that I could have the "potential" for an increased reward. The myth is that the investment is what poses the risk when in reality the risk is on the investor, not the investment. In other words, an investment that may be considered high risk for one investor may not be risky at all for another investor. The difference is the level of education around and about the investment. Know your investments at the core level before adding it to your hierarchy of wealth and things will run more smoothly for you. Risk actually equals the likelihood of loss and not the potential for gain.

Another thing I thought was true only later to realize was just another myth is that we need a degree. Specifically, that I myself needed a college degree in order to be successful. This couldn't be further from the truth either! There are many avenues for people to pursue to obtain specialized education for their chosen passion and/or profession. There is not just ONE; a degree it is just one of the ways. College isn't for everyone; business ownership isn't for everyone. Not every investment is for everyone. The chosen path should be as unique as each individual.

It seems like women hear a lot of myths growing up that affect them later. I don't see that with men as much. For instance, I grew up in a culture where we were taught daily that women and children are to be seen and not heard. That women don't have a voice. That a woman's only purpose is to serve men and bare children, and by no means were women to be educated or independent. It was a very male-dominant culture.

Fortunately, while I was raised by a mother who modeled some of the subservient cultural behavior, she also modeled strength of mind and that it is good to have an opinion as a woman. While I was never allowed to openly voice my opinions early in life, I began to develop my own opinions anyway. Taking all of this into consideration, I witnessed mothers who sometimes were able to voice their opinions and stand their ground. As a result, I had unknowingly built a foundation that I too had a voice that one day I could use to create my own life. At 17 I chose to remove myself from that culture.

Alone and uneducated, I encountered a lot of hard knocks. I married very young and was subsequently widowed, left with a beautiful daughter to raise and detach on my own. I took that role very seriously. I would raise my baby girl to be a strong woman and to be the greatest woman she could be. It was important that she value herself as a woman and that she understands that women can create for themselves, that we are strong, that we are powerful and that we have a very unique ability to listen to our inner knowing. Further I taught her that she should drive from that space, from that fire within, that fire that every single woman is born with, but all too often is snuffed out.

In short, through raising my daughter I got to re-ignite my own fire, stoke it, tend it, nurture it and follow its promptings. From that space of adversity in losing my husband and going through tough times I learned that I could provide for myself and for my daughter. In fact, I provided very well even though I had no college education, nor do I hold a degree.

You GOT THIS!

In my life's journey so far, I have worn many hats. I have experienced marriage twice, been widowed and divorced, and I've been a single mom, a business owner/partner, real estate investor, mortgage loan officer and more. While I did not think in the beginning of my adult life that it was possible to be the woman I am today, I now know that I can have anything and everything my heart desires. I know that I am a beautiful, healing, inspiring, radiant woman of light. My purpose is to lead and to create unity to bring forth a world full of peace, abundance and joy! And, yes, I really feel like this is my purpose.

Whenever I go through adversities or challenges in my personal or professional life, I go back to the basics of remembering who I am, why I am here and what I came here to do. Remembering to honor myself as a woman, how I process information, how I make decisions, and getting back to always loving myself for who I am is critical when working through challenges.

One way to assist yourself through adversities is to STOP COMPARING yourself to others! That's what I do, and it works well. I am not the person next to me, my friend, neighbor, colleague or my partner. The only thing comparing does is tear you down. Comparing is a thief of joy. It is not useful or productive. Instead, refocus on what you are committed to create for you in your life. It could be mimicking some of the habits used by the wealthy, but it is in no way comparing.

I can look back on everything I've gone through with a tremendous peace of mind. I've created the life of my dreams. I love what I do, and I have Time Freedom. It's true and some days I'm astonished. I simply get to have it all! I get to be a business professional, a mom and a partner. I get to create my own schedule. I never have to miss a school play, musical, birthday, an anniversary or miss out on the simple things we should all be able to enjoy in our lives.

If you ask me how I got to where I am today, I'd have to say creativity played a big part, surrounding myself with like-minded people and being willing to learn. Planning did too, but not just for myself. Every plan I create for clients is 100% unique, which excites my feminine energy. My innate feminine desire to nurture, love and teach is ignited when I get to add value to all of the lives I touch.

I plan to keep doing what I do today, working with clients so they can plan for a better tomorrow through financial freedom, and I won't stop there. Currently I am creating a system designed to speak to women and the way we operate, thrive and create.

Women wear so many hats that it makes it hard to sit down and educate. The system I am working on will be automated to the degree, so each person going through it gets to choose when they will take the different components. If they have time restraints, they can do the program at their own pace and still have a great outcome. If they have time restraints during daytime hours but still want to educate and plan, that works. If their time restraints are during the evenings, they can take the program during daylight hours! My goal is to create a system that can be used and implemented no matter what time of day it is being done.

In the end, my life's purpose is to create a compounding effect with the people I assist, so that what I do spreads like wild fire. I want every family and every individual to have a solid foundation built upon the 7 Principles of Prosperity, that the Perpetual Wealth Strategy becomes a household name and that the typical chosen vehicles (government-qualified plans) aren't front of mind and we get rid of the herd mentality when it comes to creating financial freedom. There are vehicles for driving wealth and freedom that have been around for hundreds of years. I want to get back to our roots by educating both men and women and inspiring them to live a better life, THEIR life.

THREE TIPS:

{1} **Read/Speak out your creation statement loudly twice a day.** That means when you wake and before you go to sleep, preferably while looking in the mirror.

[2] **Get out there and meet people!** The people you meet and lives you touch are better as a result of meeting YOU. Always remember that.

[3] **Money or fame does not make you or anyone else better than the next person.** We are all humans here on earth making choices that lead us in the direction we are going. We are where we are today as a result of our "best" choices in each moment. Everyone has their own unique path and we are all at the same basic level. Always remember that and never cower to another person simply because he/she may have more money than you. Simply observe how they

got where they are now, and if you can mimic some of their healthy habits, which will in turn add value to your life, then by all means, do so.

"Knowing how to implement various real estate investment strategies helps me create custom Mom 'n' Pop solutions, but in general, the piece I can offer that most people can't is knowledge of how the secondary market for seller financed notes works. That's where I can step in and really make a difference!"

~ Dawn Rickabaugh, Note Queen

Dawn Rickabaugh, Note Queen

From nursing to notes, not all investors' paths are the same

Dawn Rickabaugh became fascinated with notes while working as a nurse and raising children. She never suspected she would one day become known as The Note Queen, but that's exactly what happened. According to Dawn, she was 'born breech'... first mastering paper investments (notes) and then backing into property investments.

"I graduated from college with a B.S. in nursing and worked in the ER at a local trauma center," says Dawn. "Then I had kids, lots of kids, one right after the other. I became interested in exploring all sorts of strategies that would allow me to quit trading my hours for dollars, so I took all sorts of classes and courses. There were a lot of options for making money, but I kept circling back to notes."

Dawn adds that when she learned how they worked, that they were secured by real estate, she knew it was a strategy she could sink her teeth into. Over time she became a go-to expert when it came to owner financing and notes, and she now gets to help others understand how to use them to solve problems and make money. She grew slowly and steadily into the nickname she was given in 2007: The Note Queen! This is her story...

***

In the beginning when I was learning about the different ways to earn money, I was a definitely a tire kicker. I would dip my toe in and do a small deal here or there while working full-time as an ER nurse and as a mom, but I didn't commit for several years. I was afraid to pull the trigger and do a deep dive into real estate and note investing.

I leveled up in 2002 when I really had to find an art studio for my wife. The experience of buying a commercial building with seller financing

You GOT THIS!

taught me so much. I became less timid and even summoned the nerve to question attorneys who shockingly knew less than I did about how notes should be crafted.

Learning how seller financing and notes worked eventually led to me having what I call an "unfair advantage" as a real estate investor. I can often resurrect deals that other investors thoughtlessly toss in the trash. I learned the powerful benefits of carrying paper. I'm often the bank and almost never the landlord. That was my strategy for about 10 years.

In 2014, my wife and I moved to Carson City, Nevada, where it made sense to add a number of properties to our portfolio of notes. In hindsight, we did things a little backwards. Usually people do what we did in reverse. They build a portfolio of properties and then convert them to paper later on in life (through carrying paper on them, or selling for cash and using the proceeds to make private loans).

Knowing how to implement various real estate investment strategies helps me create custom Mom 'n' Pop solutions, but in general, the piece I can offer that most people can't is knowledge of how the secondary market for seller financed notes works. That's where I can step in and really make a difference!

Over time I've learned (and teach others) that there are a lot of ways to put deals together using notes. In fact, like I said, it's become my "secret weapon."

I like to say I took the "short bus" to The Queendom. It was a longer, more challenging journey than I anticipated. I definitely did not make the transition from W-2 to entrepreneur look graceful, but I was very passionate about what I was doing and I wouldn't give up. When you are focused on how you can be of service, intent on discovering your divine work – that which you're most passionate about – when you don't focus on the money and you constantly receive input from others and integrate the feedback you're getting from life, you'll eventually come into alignment. Powerful unseen forces reward bold action.

A little secret is that you have to become willing to evolve into a new person. It's not just about learning new skills. You'll need to integrate your spirituality, your relationships and all areas of your life. Truth be told, I had no idea just how much transformation I would experience as I grew into a successful full time investor. It is critical that you learn how

to hear, trust and follow your inner guidance … and lose your fear of making plenty of mistakes.

If you're not making mistakes you're playing it too safe!

I'm still learning and adding properties to our portfolio. We run three of our units as short-term rental properties. We also do a little rehabbing, which has been a steep learning curve. Our first project in town was probably too big! In hindsight I wonder how I ever thought I could pull it off, but I had learned to take one step at the time and trust my intuition. Everything I needed showed up when I needed it.

I pulled 16 used mobile homes down from South Lake Tahoe and dropped them into a mobile home park in Carson. Dealing with manufactured housing, the movers, the owners, the manager, cobbling together a rehab crew, keeping the project financed… it was a lot. But we got through it and can look back with satisfaction. We'll just call it my fast and furious entrée into the "University of Physical Assets."

In retrospect I may have done things a little differently, but it worked out fine. In the end I decided that I would never do this for someone else's mobile home park again. But I would definitely do it for my own some day! When you are dealing with mobile homes in parks, you really have to have a lot of trust in the ownership and management, because they can make or break your investment.

That deal forced me to learn new and valuable skills, positioned me in the community, and built me a team. Now I've proven to myself that given the right conditions I can easily turn $10,000 into $30,000 (or more if I carry) in a mobile home park!

If I were having a conversation with a woman just entering real estate investing I'm not quite sure what I would tell her. All I could share is what I have done. That's all I know. I might tell her that if you have a strategy down and you're good at that strategy, there's nothing wrong with sticking with it. But if you have a little extra bandwidth and can master paper and develop a deep understanding of owner financing and notes, it will be extremely profitable. Mailbox money will change your life!

With notes, it's not that hard to start with a little bit of money and learn to explode the returns. That's especially true if you're using a self-directed IRA.

You GOT THIS!

Further, I'd tell her to get in the middle of some deals! You can do anything with paper (notes) that you can do with property (real estate). You can wholesale them, rehab and flip them, buy-and-hold them, do joint ventures, etc.

Notes can be challenging, but they've been amazing for me. You might be ready to carry paper on a property you already own, or buy someone else's performing and/or non-performing notes, or become a private lender. It depends on where you're at in your understanding and in your life.

If I were to tell you how I really got into real estate investing you might be surprised. Like I mentioned before, I was an ER nurse. I worked hard. I wasn't the "Note Queen," a brand that well-meaning veterans in the industry told me wouldn't work... you'll never make it with a name like that, no one will take you seriously. They don't seem to be saying that so much now.

It all started with a vivid dream I had one night in January of 2004 in which Jesus literally pushed me over a cliff! (Very lovingly, of course. He was being sort of a prankster). Yet, I didn't fall to my death in the ravine below. Instead, I trusted the process and found myself floating in the air. Then I began to fly. I woke knowing there was a very direct and personal message for me in that dream, and that very day I gave notice to my employer.

I tried on a lot of hats. I got my real estate license, I did short sales, some hard money loans, and I was doing a lot of cold calling to find properties to buy at a discount. As I talked to hundreds of owners, especially older owners, offering them cash for their properties, they wouldn't show the least bit of interest. What they wanted was to reduce capital gains, have income for retirement and leave a good inheritance for their children.

That's when all my note training came back to me and I realized that if I could help them understand owner financing, how they could carry paper on their properties becoming a lender instead of a landlord, they would get everything they wanted and I could get more of what I wanted. Owner financing gives birth to the note business.

Once a seller agrees to carry paper for a buyer, they no longer have to manage the property and usually make far more monthly income with much less effort... and still secured by the same property they know so well. They get a hassle free stream of income without having to pay for property taxes, insurance or maintenance.

Because I was always talking about owner financing and notes in an office that was focused on cash fix and flips, I was dubbed "Note Queen" by a gay guy in the office. They always wanted to offer the sellers a huge pile of cash, and I would always say, "Why don't we ask if they'll carry?"

In those early years I was desperate to do anything that would put cash in my pocket, but with time I noticed that frequently when I did something just make a buck, it had a way of blowing up in my face. On the other hand, when I consistently followed my core passion I was much more successful and a lot happier. The experience was like peeling away layers of an onion. One by one I discarded the layers (business activities) that weren't really "me," and what was left was my authentic and right path to prosperity.

When I quite my nursing job and jumped headlong into investing, we literally risked everything. We had four kids, three dogs and two mortgages. Looking back, even though it was extremely difficult and I used up every bit of net worth we had built up to that point, I wouldn't change anything. I love my life now. What I've created and who I've become has been worth all the time, effort and stress. I am now very happy and profoundly unemployable.

People ask me about myths. We all hear a lot of things as we grow up and when we first become interested in investing, and some of those things turn out not to be true.

Without necessarily being conscious of it, one myth I entertained early on was that men were better at business than women, and that I would probably never be as good as the men in the industry.

Growing up Mormon, I was raised in a very patriarchal culture, but it was one that I loved dearly and believed in wholeheartedly until I was 30. I came from faithful, hardy, plains-crossing pioneer ancestors. When I whoops-a-daisy accidentally ended up trading in my husband for a wife, the church and I were forced to part ways. It was an excruciating process and at the time, I thought the independence I was painstakingly able to declare for myself was evidence that I had risen above that early programming.

And then Jesus pushed me.

When I quit my $100,000-a-year job and wasn't immediately a screaming success as an entrepreneur, I became profoundly insecure. I had always been good at everything… school, sports, finding work, making money, popping out babies. Things just usually came easy for me. For the first time in my life they didn't.

I was also faced with the unpleasant realization that my sense of self was heavily dependent on my job as a nurse… the stories I could tell, the money I made, the car I drove. What a shocker! It hit me hard and I vowed never again to let those sorts of things define who I was or how much I was worth as a human being. There's nothing wrong with those things, clearly, but they're not who we are.

In this state of emotional regression, I entered headlong into the world of notes for keeps. It seemed like I was the only woman at the conferences. In the mid to late '90s, it was definitely a male-dominated industry. I had heard of one or two other women in the field, but had never personally met them.

I felt vulnerable and desperate for a lot of male support. It took me a long time to reclaim an internal locus of control and take my power back. The dictionary says:

Locus of Control is the extent to which people believe they have power over events in their lives. A person with an internal locus of control believes that he or she can influence events and their outcomes, while someone with an external locus of control blames outside forces for everything.

Everyone (all the men) around me knew more than me, made more money than me, would always be more successful than me, or at least that's what I believed deep down I guess. I was severely out of balance and it took me years to gradually seduce the sense of power back inside where it belonged. I eventually proved to myself that my own intuitive guidance was typically more accurate (for me) than all the well-meaning advice I got from people around me on how to approach my business.

Remember how some people told me I was never going to make it as the Note Queen? They'll never take you seriously, they said. Well… I hope no one ever takes me seriously. In fact, I mostly hope to God I never take myself too seriously! We need to be having fun with what we're doing and be able to laugh at ourselves. I never want to end up with another ego disaster like I had the year after I first quit my nursing job.

Plus, it's a bonus that "Note Queen" comes with sort of a built-in disclaimer... I don't have to spend a lot of time convincing people that I am not a licensed attorney, tax accountant or investment advisor and that they should always do their own due diligence. Take everything I say with a grain of salt... it's for entertainment purposes only!

The power inside concept is not to say that we don't need other people. Of course we do! I will always be so very grateful for the good men and women in my life that were and are there for me at every stage and teach me so much. I readily acknowledge that I wouldn't have made it through certain critical stages of my career it if it hadn't been for a couple of very special men in my life.

Investing is best as a team sport, and so much more fun than doing it alone, but we really need a strong sense of self and clear boundaries to keep the interpersonal dynamics in our organizations and communities healthy and balanced.

If you're going to be a successful investor or any type of entrepreneur, it's important that you bring all of yourself into alignment and balance. For the most part, when you're punching a time clock you can be out of alignment, a bit grumpy, and it won't necessarily affect your paycheck. As an entrepreneur, I find that being out of alignment quickly affects my bottom line.

If you're not aligned with your true intentions and divine purpose, and if you don't have passion about what you're doing, a reason that inspires you, it will likely be a tougher road. You'll be clawing and scratching after success instead of getting in the flow and feeling like you're along for the ride.

When I first started out, I was working, working, working so hard just to close maybe 20% of the deals on my plate.

I worked my ass off over the years, learned everything I could, put in countless hours and spent many sleepless nights racking my brain for what more I could be doing. But it wasn't until I experienced a profound energetic shift that everything changed.

This is the most important concept I can share, because once someone learns about these universal laws they can manifest joyously in any and every area of their lives. The process I went through was much more important than any strategy I every learned.

Like I said earlier, it is critical that you learn how to hear, trust and follow your inner guidance. It's important to work towards a healthy balance between your sacred inner power and a sense of surrender to the divine sources and higher wisdom that lovingly surrounds you.

Ultimately, I had to overcome severe guilt, shame and merciless self-flogging. For five years, while I was making progress and learning a lot, I had very critical inner dialogue… You're a failure, look what you've done to your family! You've blown through your entire net worth and compromised your family's financial future. What are you doing? Why is it taking you so long?!! The harsh self-judgment was stopping me from receiving everything I'd been working for.

Sometime in 2009 I hit my do-or-die moment. While I had made some great breakthroughs, I just couldn't create the financial consistency needed to support our robust family life. I was out of dough. I was out of equity. I was out of room on my credit card. I was ready to surrender and I got down on my knees.

Hey God, how's it goin'? Look, I gave it my best shot. I honestly thought I was doing what I'm supposed to be doing, but I guess I was wrong. And you know what? I am tired of trying to do it my way. I don't want to be in control any more. Honestly, all I want is to know what You want me to do. Do You want me to go back to nursing? Flip burgers? Whatever You want, but I've got to do something quick… have you seen the check-book lately? Thanks. Look forward to hearing from you soon.

Inside of that very same week there were three synchronicities, three messages that came to me through other people. I got the hit to "just wait." Just wait, seriously? I mean haven't I waited long enough as it is? But, okay, whatever you say.

Because it wasn't on me, for the first time in five years all the critical self-talk fell silent. It wasn't my idea to sit back and do nothing… I was just along for the ride. I was able to forgive myself for all offenses and failures real or imagined. The inner stillness allowed me to hear my guidance. I was available to pay attention and just casually observe what was showing up, being dropped right in my lap, naturally, effortlessly.

Within four months I began building a portfolio of notes leveraging other people's money, which is great because I didn't have any of my own left. Dear old Henry Dvorken from Wichita Falls, Texas, gently held my hand through my first note transaction. I had never purchased one for myself, only brokered them off, so I was scared. He had always encouraged me to quit trying to make a fast buck and go long being an investor, not a broker or wholesaler. I was finally ready to listen.

I would keep the spread between the yield I'd bought the note at and what I had to pay my investor for the money. My very first note was a small front-end partial that I bought at a 25% yield, and I only owed my investor 15%, so I had about $50 passive income "out of thin air" without any of my own capital invested. (Of course I had a lot of blood, sweat and tears invested!)

Step and repeat.

Within 18 months I had the PITI (principal, interest, taxes & insurance) on my Southern California home covered on a passive basis, with none of my own capital invested. That was a game changer. I had created a base salary for myself that allowed me to continue to grow and expand my business and investing portfolio.

I have an unshakable inner knowing that we are much more than what we think we are in this three-dimensional world. We are capable of so much and it's easier for it to unfold when we connect to our higher power and inner guidance.

My wife and children continue to be great support and inspiration. My mother was my greatest fan, even though my antics could scare her half to death. My financial friends and all the relationships I've created along the road to The Queendom continue to be invaluable. We need connection and support. We need family, faith, vision and a network. With those there's nothing we can't accomplish.

At this point in my life I rarely do anything that isn't fun for me. It's not just about making money and building wealth. When you love what you do, you can work like a maniac and still be having fun and find deep fulfillment on a daily basis.

I get to be a hero and help people.

Let's say someone in town doesn't have enough to buy a property for cash and can't get a bank loan. They're stuck in the rent cycle. There's a chance that I can bring in a private investor or carry a note for them. A renter becomes an owner, helping to stabilize the community and money stays local instead of running off to Wall Street.

I've had agents bring me in to solve big problems on deals that were falling apart. We discuss different out-of-the-box options and before you know it, we're at the closing table. When I can save a deal and get a seller out and a buyer in to a home they really want, and get everybody paid, I'm talking pure joy.

The reason I am still here doing this is because I know my WHY. You have to know your WHY. Mine is helping families and making a difference in my community. I create refuge for my tribe. You have to get fired up thinking about your WHY. Get fired up about your vision of who you are, what you do and why it matters. These things should be very clear in your mind.

For example, yes, I buy notes to earn income, but I am also creating liquidity in the market that wasn't there before. I increase home ownership in my town, I help sellers, and I put the defibrillation paddles to languishing retirement accounts so regular people can earn enough to live on and don't end up on cat food the last few years of their lives.

The central banking financial system we have is pure evil, a fraud. The Federal Reserve needs to be abolished. It's a debt slavery system designed to control and impoverish the people. Creating financial solutions just one Mom 'n' Pop to another through liberal use of owner financing and notes is my way of unplugging from the wealth vampires of Washington and Wall Street and participating in the kind of system I can feel good about.

This year, 2019, I plan to get more intentional about creating leads in my own community. I want to build a legacy, which means I have to get better at marketing and at getting the word out about what I do. I want to buy more performing and non-performing notes as well as properties here in Carson and surrounding areas so I can create more opportunity and increase the impact on the community.

I host the Property & Paper Summit, a live two-day event in Lake Tahoe each October each. It's a very intimate venue and has been amazing for all of us. I usually sell out each year as I can only accommodate 35 attendees. It's a unique experience and I'd encourage people to sign up at PropertyPaperSummit.com for the next gathering if they're interested in learning more and connecting with like-minded people.

In order to make that event a better for those newer to the conversation, I'm in the process of creating a new digital course that will make it really fun and easy to understand the world of owner financing and notes. Stay tuned for its release by signing up at NoteQueen.com and creating a free account. You will also get notifications of Virtual Coffee, a free Q&A session I host that turns into an iTunes podcast each month.

My longer-term goal is to do more writing and spend more time outdoors skiing, cycling and backpacking. The Harley and ATVs have their place, as well! But retirement is ultimately a meaningless concept. I don't want to ever stop being involved in real estate investing and notes, but I could perhaps start experiencing these things from a different vantage point.

THREE TIPS:

[1] **Be prepared to risk everything for love, for your passion, and don't give up.** Depending on where you're at, you may or may not need to take a huge leap of faith. Believe in yourself. Be willing not only to do new things, but to become a completely new version of yourself!

[2] **Be gentle and forgiving of self and others.** Seriously, stop punishing yourself if you aren't learning as quickly or doing as many deals as others. Don't be punitive or judgmental of other people either. We are all doing the best we can!

[3] **Make sure you're in alignment with your true purpose and that you are serving others.** You are not here on the planet at this time by accident. You are here to do something only you can do and when you're on your authentic path, you will be supported in miraculous ways!

"Don't hold yourself back! Your goals will be different than another investor's goals. You have to decide for yourself what strategies are right for you and, more important, WHY you are interested in earning income through real estate investing."

~ Marietta Anderson, Real Estate Developer

Marietta Anderson, Real Estate Developer

In real estate, the sky's the limit!

As a developer that specializes in multi-unit projects and properties in Los Angeles, Marietta Anderson has a lot of knowledge to bring to the table. But it wasn't always this way. She started out slowly and sped up over time. She learned that there was no one holding her back but herself!

"I started in real estate about 10 years ago," explains Marietta. "My dream was to own apartment buildings. But that's not what I did right off the bat. At first, I sold real estate as an agent. That way I could learn the business from the foundation. I sold duplexes at that time; most of my clients were already successful investors. So, I asked every investor with whom I crossed paths how they started their business and how many properties they owned. I learned a lot with those questions! People love to talk about their successes, so it was a win-win. As a result, I learned several different business models, which helped me put together my own business model. I was excited about where I'd go next!"

Here is Marietta's story...

***

Once I got into real estate investing, I knew it was for me. Everything was so exciting and I never grew tired of learning new strategies. I started as a real estate agent and learned a lot that way. Then I started doing small deals, then bigger deals. Flash forward a few years and I'm still excited about being involved in real estate investing. If I were talking to someone new to investing, I would tell her to GO FOR IT! The sky truly is the limit!! Actually, I mentor new investors all the time and that's what I tell them.

I tell them not to be influenced by other people's fears. I also tell them to have flexible goals and business plans, because real estate changes constantly. Being flexible allows you to adapt and grow much faster.

You just can't hold yourself back! Your goals will be different than another investor's goals. You have to decide for yourself what strategies are right for you and, more important, WHY you are interested in earning income through real estate investing. There is no wrong answer.

For me, it is personal satisfaction, because when I created my business model, I created it to benefit my friends. I come from the beauty industry and most of my friends are beauticians, massage therapists and make-up artists. I wanted to show them that there is a way they could create a passive income from activities that didn't interfere with their day-to-day life and to-do lists. Once my kids started school, I gained more friends, many of whom are single mothers, and they need to know that there is a way to earn passive income so they can spend more time with their children, too. If I can open their eyes to the possibilities, it makes me happy.

One of the things that I've seen when working with my mentees is that they think they need money to invest in real estate. That's not correct! You absolutely do NOT need money to invest in real estate. What you need is to find a good deal and then the money will come. You need to talk to your friends, neighbors, relatives and other people in your life. Your sphere of influence is a great way to start in this business.

That said, it's best to get used to chatting with strangers and people you meet at networking events about private lending. That's what you need. Lots of cash investors and buyers. That's first on the list. Then when a property that fits the investor's or buyer's needs comes along (or you find it for them because you know what they like), you can feel confident in putting in an offer on the property, because you'll be able to get the money or sell the place (if it is a wholesale or flip deal).

Another myth I hear a lot is that my mentees think that it is very difficult to sell a house. Again, that's just not factual. A property may not sell overnight, but every property sells at the right price. To sell a house is not difficult; what is difficult is to come with the right evaluation, which requires the right skills. For example, you have to understand your market. It is always best to do your due diligence to make sure you are at that right price point. This is something I learned more from my days as a real estate agent than investor, but it holds true today just as it did 10 years ago!

Another thing I make sure my mentees know is the importance of building and growing a team. You're going to need other professionals as you scale your business. Believe me, investing is a business; it is not a hobby.

Teams are critical to your success down the road. However, I'll admit that the most difficult challenge I have faced in real estate is finding the right team. It has been hard to find people who are willing to work "as a team." But to grow you are going to need to surround yourself with people you can trust.

Not everyone is a team player. In fact, few are! You will need to work with architects, engineers, contractors, lenders, investors, partners, escrow officers, title officers, real estate agents, buyers, sellers, tenants, property managers, and the list goes on. The good news is every deal is different and you can test people until you find your "dream team."

Understand that when you are building your real estate investing business, you will face challenges. You will overcome adversities as you learn and earn. Your journey will not be smooth, and it shouldn't be. How else will you learn? If things always run smoothly you won't learn much. I promise.

To me, adversity is just a path for learning and growing. It's good to analyze adverse situations and challenges. Figure out what went wrong and what went right. Approach challenges as lessons. Don't look at adversity as a bad thing. It's not. It's good. It's a very good thing!

It is this perspective that helps me get through adversity much easier. Like most things in life, overcoming adversities really comes down to your view of things. Your personal perspectives and beliefs. If you keep a positive outlook and the right attitude, you can get through just about anything. You'll experience more joy and less stress as a result!

I've had a few challenges doing deals that could go down in history as the oddest adventures of all time. For example, when I was starting out as an agent, I received a call from an English investor about selling his house. He said it was up in the Hollywood hills. A couple of us from the company met with him to give him a few tips how to prepare his house for sale. He listened and everything seemed to be going well. We would sell his house; I would earn a commission. That's how it was supposed to go... but it didn't.

First, the man took our suggestions a bit too far about trimming back some trees for better curb appeal. He went the extra mile and chopped all the trees way, way back. Next thing we knew, he was in a law suit with his neighbor over the trees! So, we suggested that he have a survey conducted on the land. In the end, the trees were on his land. Unfortunately, the neighbor had built a fence, claiming the land was hers when in fact she was encroaching on our client's property. What a mess!

After some back and forth and much debate, we were able to put the house on the market. Even better, we received an offer right away. However, things took another strange turn when our client said he wanted some of his friends to stay in the house for a couple weeks. He said they were flying in from Europe and he really wanted them to stay at his place. We weren't in agreement and before we knew it the locks on the house had been changed. We had no access. Again, what a mess.

We had no recourse but to call the police. We were sure they would side with us and understand the situation, but that's not what happened. One of our client's friends lied to the police and even filed a Grand Theft charge against us! What did he say we stole? That's a great question!

You see, my husband had done some showings of that house while the visitors were there. They claimed he had stolen jewelry from them. But wait, that's not all... They also claimed that we had threatened to kill the Michelle Obama. Yes, the then-President's wife. Unbelievable! If that were the end of the story it would be a little anticlimactic. You're in luck, because the next day we were paid a very special visit at our office by none other than the Secret Service. Once they understood what was going on, things got better. In the end, not only were the squatters removed from the property; they were kicked out of the country. We learned a lot during that tough time, for example, the importance of due diligence to make sure who we are dealing with are the people who have the rights to the property and have the right to sell it. We learned not to trust so openly, too. These people were professional scam artists; they had done this type of thing before. I guess some people just have too much time on their hands!

Another time, we bought a single-family property in the West Adams area in Los Angeles with the intention of turning it into a 4-plex. We had an investor partner who was putting the money as equity. He was then our equity partner. While he should have just been the money guy who made money when we made money, he may have been a little confused about his role. You'll understand why in a few seconds.

Once we had the financing secured, we were ready to move ahead with the project. We were excited when we pulled permits and were able to start construction. Everything was moving along well... until it wasn't. We were two months away from finishing the project, the equity partner hired a new business manager. The next thing we knew, we had a group of lawyers trying to change the terms of the deal. They wanted to treat it as a loan, they wanted a $25,000 processing fee and they wanted interest on the initial investment and they wanted the equity as well!! We were in disbelief, but our agreement with the equity partner wasn't as solid as it should have been. Talk about another lesson. It was a costly one! After going back and forth with the attorneys, we got into a new agreement. However, it wasn't a great one. In fact, it cost us more than $25,000!

In the end, we sold the property and moved on. Sometimes that's all you can do. You have to be careful about the people who are in a deal with you. Make sure to check them out; don't take people at their word. Do your research, your homework, your due diligence, not only regarding the deal. Rather, research the people that you are going to be working with.

I know I sound like a broken record, but truly doing your research is a step you cannot skip in any deal. A lot of times you don't really know the people personally who are lending you the money or doing different parts of the deal. That's on you! If you do proper research to make sure your partners are who they say they are and that they have a good track record, you will be better for it.

Sometimes problems aren't in your wheelhouse to fix. But most of the time they are. Right down to making sure you pull permits and go step by step like the city wants in a rehab. If you don't, your project will be delayed and you could lose money. That's a promise.

Believe me. I know, because I've been there and done that!

We bought a house in Tujunga, California, on a big lot. It was a nice-sized lot! So, my partner and I decided to split the lot into two parcels. We would rehab the existing house and build another new house on the back lot. That's all good, but we didn't go about things in the proper manner. You see, we decided to do part of the rehab without permits. Big mistake. We didn't get away with it; permits are needed for a variety of reasons. Number one is that the structure is built correctly or changed to code. When the inspector came out to the property, big surprise, he made us tear everything down and start over. That was a costly lesson on following the rules. That said, once we did things by the book and followed the rules we could look back five months later at a beautiful house we had created. And everything was legal!

Truth is that I wouldn't trade any of the negative experiences I've had as an investor. And I wouldn't trade any of the great many positive experiences! They made me who I am today.

My biggest joy is to be able to help others create wealth, freedom and happiness through real estate endeavors. That is on the professional side of life, but that side only adds to my personal life. Because of my involvement in real estate and investing, I have the flexibility to spend more time with my family, to be a better mother and enjoy a happy, healthy life. Because I am an investor, I get to enjoy traveling with my family. I want more people to be able to do the same. Success makes this happen, so what are you waiting for? Grab a mentor... even if it's not me... and get going.

Real estate investing is not a one-woman show. Like I said, it takes a team. And you will never get to bigger and bigger goals alone. I have a great team. They deserve my full support, so one of my goals for the future is to create more passive income opportunities for my team. What that looks like exactly is a little in the air right now, but I'm working on it!

I would also like to go more environmentally green with our developments and would welcome the opportunity to build more affordable housing for low-income people. They need a leg up and I want to give that to them in sensible ways.

My main 10-20 year goal is to hold on to more rental properties to generate a more steady flow of passive income. I know people who live comfortably just from rental income, and that's where I want to be. My plan is to own hundreds of units. Maybe thousands! The rest is just icing on the cake.

My passion for real estate has really motivated me to focus on creating a "one stop shop" real estate business. In the short term I want to build my brand and
provide my clients and investors with a resource they can count on for all of their real estate needs (buying, selling, investing, consulting, management, development and construction). I am fortunate to be working with a great team and we are currently working on bringing this vision to life.

Without my team the sky might not be the limit. I'm very grateful for each and every person who helps and supports my goals and vision. I can't wait for the next leg of this wonderful journey!

THREE TIPS:

[1] **Have clear goals**. Don't fall into the pattern of trying everything or jumping from one path to the next. Sit down and write out your goals. Not just what you want to do in real estate as an investor or the strategies that most interest you, but rather WHY you want to take this journey in the first place. The clearer your intentions are, the better your journey will be.

[2] **Learn your market.** The better you understand your market, your properties and your tenants the better you will do. Bother to learn. Don't be lazy about your education.

[3] **Learn from successful people.** Don't be afraid to ask questions. A lot of times you may feel like seasoned investors will be bothered if you ask questions because you don't know something. It's quite the contrary! Seasoned investors, particularly female investors, enjoy mentoring. At least that is what I've seen time and time again. So don't be afraid of what others will think. Ask away!

"Watch out for the 'gotchas' in real estate transactions and any contracts. Get educated, stay informed and ask others to look things over for you. Put your ego aside. Get guidance when you need it and you will succeed!"

~ Kathryn Morea, Founder of Shortstaybeachrentals.com

Kathryn Morea, Founder of Shortstaybeachrentals.com

Teamwork really does make the dream work!

Southern California-based real estate investor Kathryn Morea has learned a few important things over her years as an investor. A big one is that nothing beats having a team to help you get to your goals!

"For the last 10 years I've focused on short-term rentals in southern California that I own and manage myself," says Kathryn. "I also have some out-of-state, long-term rentals that are managed by local property managers in those areas. I've come to depend on these members of my team, because it simply makes life easier. I tried wearing all the hats, but that only works for so long. To be successful in real estate investing, you need a team. It takes a lot of people to get to the good life as an investor. While you may start out doing everything yourself, you'll eventually need a good real estate agent, a real estate attorney and an estate planning attorney , contractors for construction, a public adjuster for insurance claims, a good bookkeeper and CPA , and other professionals so you can scale your business."

Sound words of advice, but then Kathryn learned these things over the years. Here is her story...

***

I have always been enamored with real estate. At just 22 years of age I bought my first single-family property in Van Nuys, California, using FHA financing and $7,000 that I inherited from my grandmother. Two years later I bought a condo. A few years after that I started acquiring properties at auctions in Southern California. Something I wish I had understood when I first started out is just how important it is to find someone who is doing what you want to do in real estate and then mirror them. If I were mentoring a young woman just starting out today, I'd tell her to get connected with like-minded people who can support her in her goals. Something magical happens when you attend different real estate meetings near you! The meetings open doors.

It's even better when you live in an area with multiple real estate clubs, so you can visit the different clubs to see which have a format and style you like. Reading, studying and taking classes about how to invest in real estate is great, but it's critical to your success to take the leap and actually do deals. Do your first and then keep going! Make offers. Buy something. Take action. That is the only way success in this field is going to happen for you.

Once you have the basics down and you've done a couple of deals, you need to find the vehicle that speaks to you and hone your skills in that area. There are so many things to specialize in – flips, notes, buy-and-hold (rental properties), mobile home parks, self-storage units, etc. Find something that your skill set works well in, then dive in and learn all you can about that niche. Find others who are doing that market segment. See if you can intern with them. You'll get seasoned more quickly using this approach.

For me, it's been all about short-term rental properties (STRs). I didn't purposely go into this area, but was willing to try it and I'm happy to say that it has worked really well for me. A couple years after quitting my job to pursue real estate full time in 2006, I found my income tight and savings dwindling, as I used it for down payments on out-of-state rental properties.

So, I stopped, took a breath and asked myself what I could do to get more cashflow out of my properties. STRs was the answer!

Around 2008, I got into the STR market by converting the dining room of my home into a private guest space, closing it off from the rest of the house. It had a private entrance, which was important. I added a coffee pot and microwave, and made the space comfortable for and appealing to travelers. The space started renting immediately and soon I was earning $2,000 a month in cashflow from that one small space! I knew I was onto something that I could repeat.

Next, I turned a tiny apartment that was also attached to my home into an STR. I waited until my regular renter's lease was up and then took action. That STR rented all the time. It was great! Each time a long-term tenant would move out of a property, I'd turn it into a short-term rental.

Because I'm a good shopper I know how to keep costs down. I hear some of the STR gurus talk about how costly it is to set up a good STR.

I disagree. I can buy good-quality sheets from Ross, furniture from Ikea and find bargains on literally everything else I need when setting up my STRs, so the overhead is not that bad.

Before I really found my niche with STRs, I tried my hand at different aspects of real estate, such as buying land at tax auctions, buying tax lien certificates, and of course long term rentals, including some outside California. Owning properties in Tennessee, Missouri, Texas, Utah and Florida proved challenging, and that's when I understood the importance of hiring the right property managers. These people can't be just anyone; they have to really understand your market, which means they need to understand the tenants' mindset and the type of property they are being hired to manage. If it's a lower-class market, the manager has to understand that people might steal fridges and can do some strange things in your properties. This is especially true of the Section 8 housing market. Fortunately, I found a great property manager for my Tennessee properties where I encounter pesky tenant issues and am always on the lookout for other great managers for my other properties.

I no longer own the Florida and Missouri properties. I have a number of single-family properties scattered around in different states, as well as some single-family properties as well as a duplex and a triplex in the Los Angeles area. I'm not looking to add to my portfolio here in Los Angeles due to rent-control and increasing regulation which makes land lording more cumbersome. When the market dips again, I might consider it, but I'm on the fence right now... unless I can figure out another way to make better cashflow!

That brings me back to the STRs I own and manage at the time of this writing.

Things are a little different in the STR community today than when I first started out. With so many hosts entering the marketplace the prices are being driven further and further down. I find that I have to provide far more superior spaces and guest services, working three times as hard as I used to, and then charge a whole lot less than I used to for the same spaces that once brought me great cashflow.

Now I have to think differently again.

What can I do with my properties to make them bring better cashflow?

The regulations around hosting STRs are also escalating, making it tougher on hosts. There are a lot more rules being placed on us than ever before. This is happening at the hands of city officials and Homeowners Associations. That is due in part to the great number of hosts jumping into Air BnB and other platforms. Call it a glut of inventory. Call it what you want, but it's playing havoc with us STR owners who've been at this a long time. That's okay though. In real estate you must be flexible. This is not a get-rich-quick game.

When I first entered real estate investing, I sort of bought into the myths about getting rich quickly and that investing is easy. I learned pretty fast that it is neither. Real estate is lucrative, but not necessarily quick. Plus, there are a lot of "gotchas." I'll get to that in a minute.

If someone were to ask me if I ever doubt my path, I'll have to say yes... sometimes. Probably the thing that makes me wonder if it's the right path for me is when I'm dealing with the bureaucracy, or insurance or guests who wreak havoc. It is those less glamorous sides of the business that can get to you! That's something I can talk a lot about.

For example, a few years ago a scammer filed a fictitious grant deed and mechanics lien against a property I was rehabbing with a partner. I subsequently bought the partner out. By transferring the title into my entity from my partner, it cancelled any title insurance that may have existed through escrow when the property were purchased. The fake grant deed clouded the title. Clearing it would take some time and effort. Multiple attorneys were baffled as to how to clear the title. That's because the entities showing on title didn't exist and there was no one to legitimately serve legally.

I contacted the police and every other agency I thought could help. That was the first step. Then I tracked down the notary who signed the deed so I could take a look at their signature book. Using the signor's driver's license, as well as Facebook and other websites, I helped locate the scammers (plural) and provided their info to the police. Over the next three years, one of the two scammers was caught, tried and convicted. The other one goes to trial very soon. The deed was clouded for three years. A judge would only void the title six months after the criminal conviction had taken place.

If we had been in escrow or in a refi situation, it would have been an even bigger disaster. That was a lot of sleuthing and stress for me to get so involved, but there was no one else who could do it. Plus, in the end I owned the property with clear title and could do something with it. You really have to watch out for unscrupulous people. Always have your radar up! You also have to beware of the "gotchas" of doing real estate, especially in creative real estate acquisitions. Understand that when you buy or transfer a property outside of escrow, you may not be getting the protections of something like title insurance.

This isn't the only time I've had to swim through unfamiliar waters. It's the "gotchas" that I mentioned earlier that can spring up like scary sea monsters at first. But you'll learn to navigate around them and handle any issues that spring up. Like insurance. I cannot stress enough how important it is to be willing to pay for good coverage.

I've learned through experiencing insurance claims that when damage occurs in a rental property that having good insurance helps you sleep at night. Be sure to check your policies often, too. You may think you have good insurance when you acquire the property, but later on when you fix it, did you revisit the insurance? At minimum, review your policies annually. That's something no one ever told me. But I learned to get my policies reviewed by other qualified professionals, such as different insurance agent or a public adjuster to look over and see if there are any glaring holes. Maybe you don't have replacement coverage, or building upgrades or something that covers for lost rent (that's huge if you're a landlord). There are so many things that you won't think about as a lay-person. It's really smart to have another agent sit down and go over your policies with you. That way "gotchas" won't getcha!

Stay in contact with your insurance agent. I cannot stress enough how important it is to make sure you and your entity/entities are covered. Have your agent add an additional insured when you switch from sole proprietor status to being an LLC. Lots of gurus will tell you to go the LLC route to reduce your liability, but they forget to tell you all the stuff that goes with that. One of those things is insurance and changes to your policy that happen as a result. Whenever you transfer a deed, such as moving a house from you personally own to having your LLC own it, please either write a new policy in the name of the LLC or add the LLC as an additional insured. I've had my insurance defense denied because my LLC was not listed when a neighbor sued us. Last week a similar thing happened to a friend. Their property was in a land trust, the tenant sued after a slip and fall, and their insurance denied coverage because the

You GOT THIS!

insurance was written in their name and the land trust was not named as an insured.

Another tip about insurance is to make sure the way you are using your property is actually what you are insured for. For example, if you do short-term rentals like me, make sure your insurance policy knows this is how your property is used. If you have vacant house insurance during a rehab and then you rent it, be sure to update the policy. By the way, some claims aren't covered if a house is vacant for over 30 days, something to be aware of with rentals. Having the appropriate policy (vacant house, short-term rental, etc.) costs more than a regular homeowner or landlord policy, but you don't want to find out that you actually aren't covered by saving money on premiums here.

And what about "public" adjusters? This is another tip regarding insurance. Hire a public adjuster to represent you if you ever have an insurance claim. Do not rely on an adjuster who is sent out by the insurance company to do the best job. I learned this the hard way.

Several years ago a pipe burst in one of our rental houses out of state. The insurance initially covered the claim and the paperwork was handled pretty quickly. Three weeks after the leak, the contractor began repairs. But in those three weeks, mold had grown. The insurance didn't want to pay because mold is an excluded coverage. I went round and round with the insurance company. Because I was connected with other investors through networking and meetings, I got some good advice. I mentioned the trouble I was having and it was recommended that I seek the assistance of a public adjuster who would represent me in the claims process with the insurance company. You need to pay that adjuster a percentage of the claim, and their percentage is higher if you bring them in after the initial claim, but they are worth it! In this tale, after another six months or so, the public adjuster was able to recover a significant amount from the insurance to cover the damage. I was not made whole, but I was a lot better off than if I didn't have the public adjuster.

Later, I actually experienced a fire in our home. A few hours after the firemen finished, a public adjuster knocked on our door. I hired him the same day. This time I already knew not to go out it alone. I'm convinced that I received two to three times as much with his help. So worth it! Most people don't know they can hire their own public adjuster. I sure do now. And so do you! (You're welcome.)

Facing adversity is just a part of doing business. Because I have a strong sense of justice, of right and wrong, I let that give me the strength to keep going no matter what. In return, I am rewarded by the ability to create and provide beautiful places that other people can enjoy. That goes for short-term rentals, long-term rentals and flips. There's just something awesome about taking something ugly and unloved and then turning it into something beautiful. While this rewards me on a professional level, the joy spills over into my personal life. Plus, real estate has given me a lot of freedom and flexibility in life that I could not find in a regular job. Sure, there may be more challenges in what I do than I would encounter in a regular job, but the rewards of knowing I have done the work and created great spaces that I have control over far outweigh the challenges! I wouldn't have it any other way; I could not and would not take a job at this point in my life.

Because I chose to become a real estate investor, I get to sleep in if I want, set my own working hours, put in time if I want doing the work in a property or I can hire out, and I can truly enjoy what I do. I'm not working for someone else, a boss or a manager. I am working for me and toward my personal and professional goals. Is there really anything better?

Like I mentioned earlier, as a real estate investor you have to remain flexible and open to change. Since the STR market has drastically changed since I first began in it, I have to look at new ways to earn cashflow. As a result, I am reevaluating some of my long-term investment properties and other investments, looking at changing some of the vehicles to create more cashflow.

Right now, my real estate income is mostly focused on short-term rentals that I manage myself. As I get older, I see this migrating into more stable long-term rentals that require less energy from me. My 10-year plan is to own residential rental inventory that provides $100K (or equivalent at that time) in passive cashflow per year.

Further, I am looking at the opportunity of partnering with others, which is something I have done very little of in the past. In the beginning, my now ex-husband was my partner. He did not want to have any other partners or joint ventures. We still own business and property together, and the property has done well for us.

I am open at this stage in my life to perhaps partnering with someone if the numbers work and it's something that interests me. I know I will need to do my due diligence and choose wisely, as I've heard many horror stories of things going wrong with partnerships. But I've also seen some wonderful collaboration and joint ventures that worked really well, so I know it's possible.

If you find people who are hungry and motivated, they may be great partners. Being a solo act works only for so long. You're going to get tired.

Today I see partnering as a chance to expand my portfolio in new ways and it's exciting. Partnerships can work if you choose the right partners. Besides, being the lone wolf can get lonely. Networking and partnering would solve that for me. It would offer a lot more support than always going it alone, too.

One of my mistakes historically was doing everything myself. For example, I've learned to do tiling, painting and all sorts of odd jobs involved in a rehab. While it's always good to try your hand at these tasks, because you will learn what goes into them and can truly appreciate the labor involved, it's a far better use of your time to hire people who do these things for a living. Likely they are much better at the job and things will run more smoothly. Spend your time more efficiently as the decision-maker, the landlord and the business owner!

I'm finding potential partners at real estate networking and educational events. For example, WREN hosts different events and has several chapters. Even if I don't partner with people I meet at these and other investing events, I can find support at these events. Like people I can run ideas by, or other investors who can tell me if I'm missing something in a deal or strategy. These "financial friends" come in handy. They give great advice and guidance. I'm all ears!

These like-minded individuals also help me stay more positive. While I'm really good at turning negative energy into positive action, it's great to be able to pick up the phone and talk to someone if I need a dose of motivation or positive energy. These people can help keep me from falling into the shiny object syndrome that comes with the territory of investing. There are so many ways to earn income, passively and actively, from real estate investment strategies that it can get you spinning in too many directions. By having a good support system that you build over time with other investors, you can thwart the emotions that might drive you to try too many strategies at one time.

THREE TIPS:

[1] **Watch your money.** It's your bottom line. No one is going to care as much as you do about your money. Stay on top of what's going on (vacancy, maintenance, bookkeeping). Stay ahead of financial issues. Check your bank balances. Make yourself accountable. (Hire a bookkeeper and/or accountant as you grow your business.)

[2] **Get educated; stay educated.** Attend workshops, read books, listen to podcasts, watch videos about investing and subscribe to online forums. This is not something you get to stop just because you're more seasoned as an investor. There is always something new to learn. A great way to do this is to attend lots of networking events around real estate in your area.

[3] **Get connected to like-minded people and stay connected.** Become a member of your local real estate investing club(s), like WREN, and join local forums so you can share resources and enlist the help of others. There are many ways to connect with other investors. Meetup.com is a good place to start your search. Get on the email lists of various people who host local real estate investing events and workshops. Then you are less likely to miss one!

Conclusion

Now that you've read about the journeys of 11 women and true rock stars in real estate investing, are you ready to get on your own path to success? What are you waiting for? No one is stopping you but, well, you!

Whether you are new to real estate investing, just kicking the tires to see if participating in deals is right for you, or you've been doing real estate investing for a while and are ready to up your game, all I can say is...

EXCELLENT! Become a member of WREN! Here's what membership in this women-only organization brings you:

1. **Entrance to Local Chapter Meetings** – You can't beat the unique networking opportunities that take place at these events.

2. **Training Videos and Other Related Content** – You gain insights from real estate investing professionals and our sponsors that would be difficult to find elsewhere.

3. **Recordings of Our Meetings** – This is more like a Chapter-level library of information! (If you can't make the meetings, you can find time to watch/listen to the recordings.)

4. **Access to Helpful National and Local Real Estate Investing Resources** – Think of this as WREN's "Angie's List" of resources, because it gives you direct access to WREN partners and affiliates (REI Clubs, workshops, need guidelines)!

5. **Discounts at major retailers** – These include retailers like, Sherman-Williams, Office Depot and more!

6. **Special Discounted Member Pricing** – We host a number of real estate investing educational seminars and workshops. As a WREN member, you gain access to early bird pricing and other discount pricing on these events. (This is a massive value. Just ask any woman who has attended one of our killer annual events. She will tell you!!)

7. **Access to All Our "Ignite" Videos** – That's the name of our annual event. Whether you attend or not you can benefit from the recordings. That way you won't miss a beat.

You also get to be a part of something really special. Join us!

Infinite heart and real estate business badassery – that's what WREN is all about.

Won't you join us?! Learn more. Visit www.WrenInspires.com!

Contact the featured experts

(In order of appearance in this book.)

Deborah Razo
Real Estate Entrepreneur / Coach / Founder, Women's Real Estate Network

Website: www.WRENinspires.com
Email: drazo@WRENinspires.com
Phone Number: 818.843.7771
Linked in:https://www.linkedin.com/in/deborahrazo/
YouTube: https://tinyurl.com/yyov97m3
Facebook:facebook.com/wreninspires
Instagram: instagram.com/wreninspires

Jennifer Maldonado
Real Estate Entrepreneur / Raising Capital Strategist

Website: www.jenmaldonado.com
Email: jen@jenmaldonado.com
Phone Number: (424) 230-3558
LinkedIn: https://www.linkedin.com/in/jenmaldona-do-cintron/
YouTube Channel: Jen Maldonado-Cintron

Iris Veneracion
Real Estate Entrepreneur / Flipper & Holding Companies

Website: REInvestClub.com
Email: IrisV@REInvestClub.com
Phone Number: 714-265-7676

Founder of real estate networking community, Invest-Club in Southern California and her accountability and mentorship program: 60-Day Challenge! 60DayChallengeOnline.com

You GOT THIS!

Kaaren Hall
CEO, UDirect IRA
Founder – Orange County Real Estate Investors' Association"
www.OCREIA.com

Website: www.UDirectIRA.com
Email: khall@udirectira.com
Phone Number: 714-831-1866
Address: 8 Corporate Park, Suite 210, Irvine, CA 92606

Christina Suter
Ground Level Consulting / REI Advisor

Website: www.GLIvestor.com
Email: Christina@GLIvestor.com
Phone Number: 310 463-5942
LinkedIn: linkedin.com/in/christinalsmith
Facebook: facebook.com/GroundLevelConsulting
Media: http://youtu.be/l46cdhCcIqE

Host of "Ask Christina First" On Amazing Women of
Power Radio Network WWW.AWOPTalk247.Com.
Hear me every Thursday at 8am PST

Terri Garner and Alia Ott-Carter
Co-founders of Investors In Action

Website: InvestorsinAction.com
Email: terri@investorsinaction.com
Email: alia@investorsinaction.com
Phone Number: 844-462-2846

Jennie Steed

You GOT THIS!

Wealth Strategist & Financial Educator, Paradigm Life

Website: JennieSteed.com
Email: jsteed@paradigmlife.net
Phone Number: (801) 557-6450

Dawn Rickabaugh
Note Queen

Email: Support@NoteQueen.com
Website: www.NoteQueen.com and
www.PropertyPaperSummit.com

Join her Virtual Coffee on iTunes!

Marietta Anderson
Real Estate Developer / The Ando Group

Email: marietta@theandogroup.com
Phone Number: (323)363-7597
DRE#01874132

Kathryn Morea
Airbnb Superhost, Homeaway Premier Partner

Real estate investor focused on short term rentals, fix
& flips, and buy & hold investments.
Website: Shortstaybeachrentals.com
Email:Kathryn.morea@gmail.com

Get Connected

Receive resources for buying this book:
Go to
www.WRENinspires.com/YouGotThis

WREN
WOMEN'S REAL ESTATE NETWORK
www.WRENinspires.com

Made in the USA
Columbia, SC
03 March 2020

88652750R00078